D1161710

REMAKING THE
CONQUERING HEROES

REMAKING THE CONQUERING HEROES

The Social and Geopolitical Impact of the Post–War American Occupation of Germany

John Willoughby

palgrave

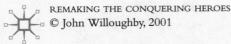

REMAKING THE CONQUERING HEROES
© John Willoughby, 2001

All rights reserved. No part of this book may be used or reproduced in any manner whatsoever without written permission except in the case of brief quotations embodied in critical articles or reviews.

First published 2001 by
PALGRAVE
175 Fifth Avenue, New York, N.Y.10010 and
Houndmills, Basingstoke, Hampshire RG21 6XS.
Companies and representatives throughout the world

PALGRAVE is the new global publishing imprint of St. Martin 's Press LLC Scholarly and Reference Division and Palgrave Publishers Ltd (formerly Macmillan Press Ltd).

ISBN 0-312-22951-8 hardback

Library of Congress Cataloging-in-Publication Data

Willoughby, John, 1949–
    Remaking the conquering heroes : the social and geopolitical impact of the early
    American occupation of Germany / John Willoughby
        p. cm.
    Includes bibliographical references and index.
    ISBN 0-312-23400-7
    1. United States—Armed Forces—Germany—History—20th Century.
    2. Germany—History—1945-1955.   3. Sociology, Military—United States—
History—20th Century.   4. United States—Military policy.   I. Title.

UA26.G3 W55 2000
940.53'38—dc21   00-062605

A catalogue record for this book is available from the British Library.

Design by Westchester Book Composition

First edition: February, 2001
10 9 8 7 6 5 4 3 2 1

Printed in the United States of America.

To Mary Ann and Zachary

Contents

Preface and Acknowledgements

This small book has an extraordinarily long history. I first had the idea of writing a manuscript on the American occupation of Germany in the late 1980s. At that point, I was attracted to this subject both as an economic historian interested in understanding the institutional roots of the postwar European expansion and a Marxist political economist who had intensively studied the Leninist theory of imperialism. My dissatisfaction with the teleological claims embedded in this analytical framework had led me to emphasize in my earlier works the importance of constructing historically contingent analyses of contemporary nation-state conflict. Postwar Germany seemed to be an ideal location for such a study. Four workplaces (Washington, D.C.; Cairo, Egypt; Lexington, Virginia; and Sharjah, United Arab Emirates) and twelve years later, the work is finally ready to be published.

I was, of course, well aware that investigating the American role in postwar Germany was an area that had already been intensively studied by scholars of politics and history. It is no exaggeration to claim that the postwar division of Germany constitutes the defining moment for the 50 years of European history that followed. My focus, however, was to be on the view of this process from the grassroots. Consequently, I decided to study the early economic documents produced by American officers working in Berlin almost immediately after the collapse of the Nazi regime.

It is impossible to sift through the documents of this period without noticing that a good portion of the chaos that existed in Germany at this time was not a simple product of emerging Soviet–American tension or German criminality. Rather, Americans in command of the occupation government constantly worried about the behavior of their own soldiers charged with carrying out occupation policy. A dispassionate reader of these documents also encounters accounts of bureaucratic disarray, confusion, and venality within the occupation government itself that prevented the implementation of the most straightforward policies. A study I thought would culminate in a monograph on the economists of the occupation government turned into this more sprawling investigation of the transformation of the occupation Army and the effect of this process on American policy toward Germany.

I soon discovered that my initial findings were not new. Between the late 1940s and late 1970s, a small group of American historians who had served in the occupation government wrote rather jaundiced accounts of the performance of the U.S. military during the late 1940s. These narratives never received the attention they deserved. Instead, the best-known histories of this period focused on explaining intensifying Soviet-American conflict, either from mainstream or revisionist perspectives. In these works, documents and sources associated with the main foreign policy actors in Washington were mined thoroughly, but the more disorganized collection of military records in the Suitland, Maryland, archives remained underutilized.

The attempt by one trained in economics to undertake a social historical investigation of the early American occupation of Germany is not without its perils. This is especially the case because I make two claims that could reorient the historiography of this era: that the experience of the occupation Army shaped U.S. policy toward Germany and thus changed the parameters of the Cold War, and that the American military emerged from the postwar occupation a transformed, domesticated institution paradoxically more capable of projecting its power throughout the globe. The attempt by an economist who is not an academic specialist on Germany to deploy political theory, diplomatic and military historical analysis, social historical investigation, and even literary criticism to support these arguments is destined to annoy many erudite readers. I am well aware that I could have more extensively consulted important archives, relied more heavily on German academic work, and collected oral historical accounts of this period. My main defense against these complaints is that further historical investigation was subject to significant declining marginal returns. I think I have the story right and welcome efforts to verify and/or rebut the arguments of this narrative.

This project also required the indulgence of my academic colleagues. Most departments of economics would not have been sympathetic to the efforts of a colleague who had just received tenure to abandon the discipline and attempt to write a historical work. It is one of the academy's little secrets that there are hardly any incentives for a specialized department to encourage interdisciplinary work. I have, however, been lucky to be associated with the Department of Economics at American University. The heterodox nature of this institution provided me the necessary cover to continue working on this subject for more than a decade. I particularly want to thank my colleagues in the Political Economy program of the Economics Department: Robert Blecker, Maria Floro, Robin Hahnel, Alan Isaac, Mieke Meurs, Larry Sawers, and Jon Wisman. Professor Howard Wachtel, also of the Economics Department of American University, was a special source of encouragement. He read earlier versions of this manuscript and encouraged me to submit it to a variety of academic publishers. His support is much appreciated.

In addition, I am happy to acknowledge the occasional financial support of the College of Arts and Sciences of American University and thank our former Dean, Professor Betty Bennett, and our present Dean and Associate Dean, Kay Mussell and Virginia Stallings. The College also gave me the opportunity to teach in and serve as Director of the American Studies Program at American University. Brett Williams's willingness to introduce to me the basic literature of American Studies and her enthusiastic support of my work was very important to me.

It is likely that this research project would never have been launched without the support of the Deutsche Akademische Austauschdienst. This worthy organization sponsored a summer trip to Berlin in 1988. There, I revived my college-level German at the Goethe Institute and breathed the curiously heavy but liberated air of caged-in West Berlin.

Many other academic colleagues also provided assistance and support for this project. Bob Beisner, Mark Grandstaff, Michael Kazin, Peter Kuznick, and Melvyn Leffler all gave me useful pointers that improved sections of this manuscript. My work on sex and the American occupation was greatly strengthened by the comments of Eileen Boris, Maria Hoehn, and anonymous reviewers for the *Journal of Military History.* I would like to acknowledge the enthusiastic support of political theorist Cynthia Enloe. Her work on gender and international relations is one of the important inspirations of my work. In addition, her colleagues in the United Kingdom, Ken Booth and Richard Purslow, also provided me with useful support and editorial suggestions. Finally, Dana Frank of the University of California at Santa Cruz read important parts of this manuscript and helped me to significantly reorganize the way I have presented my findings.

It is impossible to do any effective research without the support of librarians. I always got the impression while working in these extraordinary places of study that the archivists I worked with knew more about the subject than I did and that it might be a good idea if we switched positions. I thank all those who provided assistance to me over these years—especially the librarians from the National Archives in Suitland, Maryland, and the staff of the George C. Marshall Library in Lexington, Virginia.

The bulk of this manuscript was finished in Lexington, Virginia, an ideal place to complete this research. The Virginia Military Institute (VMI) hosts an impressive collection of documents pertaining to the career of General George C. Marshall. The Department of History at VMI also proved to be a very stimulating and able group. I would especially like to thank Professor Bruce Vandervort, friend and colleague. As editor of the *Journal of Military History,* he was able to introduce me to important literature I would otherwise not have been aware of. He read the entire manuscript carefully and encouraged me to submit this work for publication. His criticisms and support were invaluable.

The final preparation of the manuscript was completed in at the new American University of Sharjah in Sharjah, United Arab Emirates. It would have been very difficult to complete this task without the able clerical assistance of the secretary of the Department of Arabic, Humanities and Social Sciences, Mrs. Ermita Rante. Deans Samih Farsoun and Robert Cook of the College of Arts and Sciences encouraged me to complete this project as did the Chancellor of the American University of Sharjah, Dr. Roderick French. Their willingness to support a research project in the midst of founding a new university is much appreciated.

Eventually, of course, manuscripts that are completed must be published or be subject to the "gnawing criticism of rats" or computer viruses. Authors must rely on the sympathy and support of editors who have the difficult task of gauging the worth of a project, as well as its marketability. I was lucky to eventually find Palgrave and its editor, Karen Wolny. I also appreciate the efforts of her efficient and friendly assistants, Amy Reading and Gabriella Pearce.

Finally, this work would literally not have seen the light of day had it not been for the suggestions and encouragement of my wife, Dr. Mary Ann Fay. She lived with this manuscript from its birth to its completion. Her skills as a professional historian and editor forced me to condense and sharpen my ideas. The book is much better because of her support. It is for this and other much more important reasons that I dedicate this work to her and our son Zachary.

Whoever in Washington takes responsibility for placing a major American armed establishment anywhere beyond our borders, should remember that he is not thereby creating just an instrument of American policy—he is committing himself seriously to the insights, interests, and decisions of a new bureaucratic power structure situated far from our shores and endowed with its own specific perspective on all problems of world policy; and to this extent he is resigning his own power of control over the use to be made of America's resources in the process of international life.

—George Kennan, *Memoirs.*
London: Hutchinsons of London, 1968: 372.

Introduction

The Historical Significance of the Rise of American Martial Tourism in Germany

T he great turning points in twentieth-century world history have come in those relatively short five- to ten-year periods that have followed the conclusions of great conflicts. This is a time when victors and vanquished alike consider the costs of their recent struggles. It is a time of popular longings for radical reform and a return to "normalcy." Given this political schizophrenia, wartime leaders of victorious nations with systems of parliamentary democracy are peculiarly vulnerable to the discontent of their citizens. Woodrow Wilson, Winston Churchill, and George Bush are the most spectacular examples of this popular disdain. Only the rigidity of the American political calendar saved Harry Truman from a similar fate after World War II.

The social and political stresses of the immediate postwar era can be traced to the combustible combination of war weariness and the need for institutional reforms. Even if the vast majority of a society merely wishes to return to allegedly halcyon prewar days, all the institutions of military mobilization and economic and political control have to be dismantled. While the dismantling itself is not particularly difficult, managing the social dislocations and economic imbalances that follow is.

In fact, the demands for institutional reforms are more complicated than dismantling wartime institutions. The trauma of war leads policymakers, soldiers, and civilians to search for explanations of the catastrophe. Because of this, few wish to recreate a past that may lead to war again. On the other hand, historical evaluation rarely culminates in political consensus. After World War I and World War II, the politics of both communism and anticommunism in the West intensified. This and more modest disputes between conservatives and liberals were not simply arguments over internal reform. Domestic political conflict was nearly always closely linked to sharply differing conceptions of a nation's place in a reconstituted world.

The acute contradictions of postwar eras place particular stress on a nation's military institutions. In the United States, the conclusion of World War I led to the return of a relatively small military designed to intervene in the Caribbean basin and to exert control over the Philippines and Pacific basin. Woodrow Wilson's more interventionist global perspectives would have required a more robust military, but this vision foundered on opposition to the League of Nations.

During World War II, the military's projected role, after the war, was uncertain. On the one hand, there was a general establishment consensus that the United States would have to take on global responsibilities after the defeat of Germany and Japan. At the very least, it was understood that the military would have to occupy Japan and reassert control over the islands of the Pacific. On the other hand, the American role in a reconstituted Europe was not so certain. Would it be necessary to occupy Germany for a short or a long period? What would be the functions of the military during such an occupation? Would there be a military presence in other nations of Western Europe? What would be the connection between military command and the emerging United Nations? Would the American military replace financially stressed British forces in the colonial world? Would the American public support the creation of a large permanent standing Army for the first time it its history? Given all these questions, it was not at all clear how large the postwar American military budget would be.

We now know that the aftermath of World War II witnessed the beginning of a singular phenomenon in postwar American life—a large, peacetime standing Army. Since the late 1940s, millions of young Americans of modest means have traveled to military bases in Europe and Asia. Some have stayed for short tours of duty, but others have encamped for much longer periods of time. Whole American families have relocated, formed, and collapsed in the peculiar setting of the military base. During this period, the largely male part of this contingent served as soldiers, but, for long periods of the Cold War, there was little fighting to be done. Instead, the personnel and their families served as martial tourists, symbolizing the American government's willingness to make war in Western Europe and East Asia if allied territories were threatened. Through their participation in the Army, ordinary Americans implicitly supported and indeed symbolized this enormous expansion of United States power.

Now that, after a half-century, the Cold War has come to an end, it is appropriate to try to understand the ways in which the institutions of occupation were formed. This study starts from the premise that the creation of those American institutions that implemented foreign policy during the Cold War did not simply stem from the logic of superpower conflict between the United States and the Soviet Union. U.S. institutions and the policies that projected U.S. power abroad also evolved in response to more mundane problems of social control and organizational capability. The creation of a large U.S. military force as a seemingly permanent army of occupation in Germany required the policy centers in Washington to resign some of their own power of control—not only to the American military but to the emerging moderate political establishment of the new West German government. This is the first theme of this book.

This dispersal of influence, however, did not just affect policy. The American military itself changed dramatically in response to its postwar tasks. It is commonplace to note that the influence of the United States within the worlds of economics, politics, and culture grew enormously after World War II. Scholars have often emphasized the impact of a hegemonic United States on societies falling within its sphere of influence. On the other hand, historians and contemporary social scientists have devoted less attention to the reciprocating impact on American institutions of the U.S. presence overseas. Using this framework to understand the evolution of the U.S. military is this book's second goal.

Significant changes in policy and the institutions designed to implement these new initiatives required one more important shift. The culture or the ways in which policymakers and ordinary people thought about the world also had to evolve. In particular, the military needed to build new frameworks, more inclusive of all Americans, for understanding the Army and which constructed sustainable interactions with populations living in close proximity to new military bases. Understanding this rise of an expanded and more all-encompassing familial military culture is this book's third goal.

The immediate postwar period in Germany (1945-48) is an ideal historical setting for the exploration of these political, institutional and cultural issues. Germany has always been one of the three key locations for the placement of American military "assets" overseas.[1] In fact, Germany is the site in Europe where the policy of placing large numbers of troops as martial tourists began. From the vantage point of the late eighties and early nineties, the American effort in Germany has generally been judged to be successful. Daniel Nelson argues that the presence of American troops has strengthened the German-American alliance. "The huge American military presence in West Germany contributed to an ever-deepening web of social relationships between American military personnel and the German population, which had the effect of reinforcing the political and alliance relationship.[2]

During late 1945 and 1946, however, it was by no means obvious that the American presence could be sustained. The execution of this strategic program depended on the acquiescence of the American population to this use of resources at the expense of other possible state initiatives. At the close of World War II, many believed that the American population only wished to focus on domestic problems.[3] In fact, there was some concern that the soldiers themselves would not agree to stay in Europe or Asia after the war. In early 1946, there were unprecedented GI demonstrations in the Pacific and Germany in favor of the rapid demobilization of the Army.

This stunning event forcefully added the voices of disaffected soldiers to a growing chorus of harsh criticism from mainstream journals and newspapers. In many cases, opinion-makers bitterly denounced the occupation policies pursued in Germany, as well as the behavior of high- and low-ranking American soldiers. The critiques were not particularly coherent or constructive, but they did greatly worry those charged with carrying out American policy.

To make matters worse, Washington and the other occupying powers experienced great difficulty in agreeing on the appropriate policy to be pursued toward a defeated Germany as well as on how to implement those measures already agreed to. These confusing conditions further demoralized the occupation authorities. As General Lucius Clay himself notes: "We were creating a situation that was hopeless. We were preventing, not helping, the recovery of a country we had defeated, but at the same time paying for its deficits to keep it alive."[4]

Because of these circumstances, the historians who have written about this epoch have little to say that is kind to Washington policymakers or to the occupation soldiers. Historian Edward N. Peterson perhaps most starkly summarizes the cynical view of those who have most closely studied the early occupation period: "The study of the occupation should be a humbling experience to those who regard themselves as a superior race of people."[5] What makes this assessment more compelling is that Peterson and many of the other important analysts of this period were themselves officers or soldiers in the military government.

We are often taught that the Truman era was a period in which a determined and clear-sighted American political leadership forged a new role in the world for itself. Reference to this heroic epoch is commonplace in American political discourse. Yet, the studies of the early postwar period of Germany lead us to far different conclusions. Instead of political clarity, we find disarray. Instead of generosity, we find venality. Instead of forthright courage, we find dithering.

None of these conclusions will be new to the professional historian of this era, but few studies have linked the formation of "high" foreign policy to the "low" concerns of Army officials attempting

to control the base drives of their fellow officers and enlisted men.
Even fewer works have attempted to explain how the cynicism so
pervasive in the immediate postwar era became transformed into the
naive celebration of the American century that characterized the
Eisenhower era.

It is this book's intention to connect these political and cultural
concerns to the *social* conditions facing that institution most directly
involved in carrying out U.S. policy in Europe—the United States
Army. It is time for the social historian and the student of American Studies to enter the fields of diplomatic and military history—
in which the methodology remains the careful perusal of
documents generated by officials doing great or horrible things.
Such studies remain important, but if we are to understand how the
institutions of the Cold War emerged and why they remain with us
after the Cold War has ended, we need to consider the social and
institutional origins of the postwar world. If, in our new era of transition, we are to reassert, "control over the use to be made of America's resources in the process of international life,"[6] we need to
understand the ways in which the evolution of our politics, institutions, and culture all intertwined during this most significant transi-
tional period in twentieth-century American history. The purpose
of this work is to begin this ambitious enterprise by focusing on the
remaking of America's World War II conquering heroes.

Chapter I

The Collapse of the World War II Army

The Global GI Demonstrations of January 1946

January 1946 was not a good month for the United States Army. On January 9, 10 and 11, a series of demonstrations by ordinary GIs throughout the world demanded the speedy demobilization of combat veterans. The biggest demonstrations were in Manila, Philippines where as many as 20,000 soldiers participated. There were also mass meetings and protests in Honolulu, London, Paris, Frankfurt, and Berlin.

Life magazine gave particularly intense coverage to the demonstration in Paris, which attracted up to 1,000 soldiers at very short notice. The soldiers linked arms as if they were French protestors and marched from the Arc de Triomphe to the U.S. embassy. This was a wonderful photo opportunity for the *Life* editors, and the speeches themselves were of great interest. Sergeant George A. Black spoke to the assembled GIs and asked, "Why does the Army treat us like children. . . ?" "Why the continual lies about our status?" *Life* noted, however, that the American GIs in Paris were not completely unified. When Sergeant Black said that, "The generals are doing the best they can for us,' the attentive crowd booed lustily."[1]

The demonstrations in Frankfurt were less dramatically staged, but the impact was more troublesome. The *New York Times* reported that United States troops "clamored to be returned home" outside

Commanding General Joseph McNarney's headquarters in Frankfurt as well in Berlin and elsewhere in Germany. According to a "high ranking United States officer, [the result was that] the recent demonstrations . . . have done more than anything else to lower the prestige of the United States in the eyes of the German population and weaken the authority of the military government."[2]

The *Times* report ominously suggested that this sign of disunity would encourage the rebirth of the Nazi resistance movement (which showed no signs of existence after the first few months of VE Day). This impending catastrophe was blamed on the junior officers' failure to keep their charges busy while explaining to them the purpose of the occupation. The *Times* report noted that, "The average enlisted man is unaware of the potentialities for danger in Germany. He sees only a listless, subservient population and meets only accommodating women."[3] This was not the first or last time the "average Joe" had a more accurate assessment of actual conditions than hyperventilated journalists.

U.S. Policy toward Occupied Germany in the Early Postwar Days

Despite the unnecessarily apocalyptic tone of the *Times* article, there was real cause for concern about the state of the American occupation army in Germany. When the United States Army occupied the western and southern sections of Germany during the spring of 1945, the mission seemed clear: decartelize, demilitarize, denazify, and democratize. Through this "4–D" policy, the occupation authorities aimed to: eliminate the industrial monopolies, which were thought to have been one pillar of Prussian authoritarianism; destroy Germany's economic potential to wage war; imprison or isolate the supporters of the national socialist state, or both; finally, win over the German people to techniques of democratic governance. As the Army's orientation pamphlet for soldiers entering into Germany stated: "You are going to be fighting with ideas instead of guns, laws instead of tanks, control measures and policing instead of bombs. But the ultimate goals are the same—the complete stamp-out of Nazism and fascist ideas, and the re-education of the Germans to the advantages of a decent, responsible self-government."[4] Given the complexity of this task, there was little illusion that the United States could pull out of Germany at any early date.

The means for the punishment of many Germans and the restructuring of German society also seemed, at first glance, to be clear and straightforward. First, the Germans would be expected to follow the rules and regulations of the occupation government. Second, the American GIs in Germany were expected to keep Germans at arms length, but behave correctly and according to law in order to provide a "democratic example." Third, the U.S. government would only provide assistance to prevent "disease and unrest." Otherwise, the German people could expect no help in rebuilding their country or in paying reparations to the victims of Nazi aggression. Finally, the German economy would be constantly monitored in order to ensure that it could not be easily transformed for war production.

These goals and policies are far from the vision we normally have of America's postwar beneficence, and it would be wrong to suggest that there was a clear consensus among American policymakers about how Germany should be treated after the war.[5] Nevertheless, it is fair to say that, during the summer of 1945, the dominant attitude in Washington toward the Germans was punitive, not forgiving. Such an attitude is not surprising. During July and early August 1945, the "Big Three" leaders of the Soviet Union, the United Kingdom, and the United States met to consider the future of Germany. Dictator Joseph Stalin, Prime Minister Winston Churchill, and new and inexperienced President Harry Truman initially headed the conference. Midway through its proceedings, however, Churchill withdrew in the wake of the Conservative Party's dramatic electoral defeat by the Labor Party, and the new Prime Minister Clement Atlee replaced him. This interruption did not derail the partial consensus that emerged at Potsdam. The leaders agreed that Germany should remain unified, but ruled as an occupied country by the newly constituted Allied Control Council.

It was agreed that occupation authorities would direct the dismantling of machinery and other capital equipment that made Germany's war-making ability possible. In addition, occupied Germany would have to make significant reparation payments to the Soviet Union and other victims of Nazi aggression. The American side insisted that it would extend no loans or grants to Germany in order to facilitate the paying of reparations. The leaders agreed that some of the allegedly surplus capital equipment in the Western zones would be shipped to reparation recipients. In addition, the Potsdam agreement implicitly permitted the Soviet Union to extract the bulk of its reparations from the forced labor of prisoners of war and from the capital equipment of its own occupation zone in the East.

Eventually, the "Big Three" hoped that Germany would emerge as a subordinated nation-state. Strict unified supervision by the Allied Control Council would allow Germany to be economically self-sufficient, but militarily weak. Stalin, Atlee, and Truman left the articulation of specific policies for Germany to the Allied Control Council. In addition, France was given a relatively small zone of occupation along its Eastern border with Germany and allowed to participate in the Control Council as a full partner. Each country had veto power over all decisions taken in Berlin, and the actual administration of Germany devolved to the four separate occupation armies in their respective zones. Although the Potsdam agreement envisaged a neutral, demilitarized, unified Germany, this last conference of the leaders of the World War II allies actually laid the basis for the 50–year division of Germany.

The punitive decisions of Potsdam were not just based on an emotional reaction to the enormous losses of World War II. Officials also developed a particular reading of recent history, which suggested that Germany had to be strictly controlled. The occupation pamphlet that incoming soldiers read made these historical lessons particularly clear when it listed the ten key mistakes of the post–World War I period.

1. Only seven percent of German soil was occupied.
2. The occupation armies left too soon.
3. Germany was allowed to keep its army.
4. The Americans helped Germany rebuild its industry so that it could pay reparations.
5. The Americans gave financial aid.

6. Self-government was permitted too soon.
7. The staff corps of the German Army was not abolished.
8. Germany was allowed to try its own war criminals.
9. Wilson's plan for the League of Nations was never implemented successfully.
10. The occupation authorities were duped into believing that Germans had really reformed.[6]

The Americans wanted to believe that they were now taking measures that would reverse the too kind policies of the post–Versailles period. Every sector of Germany would be occupied. The Army would not leave soon. The German Army would be destroyed and its staff corps dismantled. Major war criminals would be tried by the Allies. The United Nations would function effectively. The German people would receive no reconstruction aid, and they would be viewed with suspicion for a long time to come. The occupation pamphlet attempted to steel the soldiers for this task by reminding them of German war atrocities:

> After six years of propaganda, you are going to be surprised when you see your first Germans. . . . Just as German cities are apt to remind you of America, so will the people remind you of Americans. . . . Central heating is typical of Germany, but so was Buchenwald. German cleanliness is typical—so much so that they tried to make soap out of human bodies. . . . That isn't being like Americans. . . . As an American you won't want to convict people on the basis of things you didn't see yourself, but this is one time when you have to.[7]

The writers of this important orientation pamphlet do not clearly specify the American character that needed changing. The implication is that the Army feared the average soldier would be reluctant to implement a punitive policy toward Germans, who could use their European sophistication to seduce the naive, innocent GI. The literature of this time clearly suggests that Germans might represent an attractive ideal to many American soldiers because of German industriousness, cleanliness, and, perhaps even more important, blondness. The early advocates of a policy that treated the bulk of the German population as Nazi collaborators feared that American troops would fail to implement the harsh occupation policy rigorously enough. The demoralization evident in the January 1946 demonstrations did threaten to undermine the punitive mission of the U.S. Army. There were real reasons for Washington policymakers and Army Command to worry.

Confusion and Disarray Within the Occupation Army

The final disintegration of Adolf Hitler's Germany on May 6, 1945, found 1.6 million American troops in Germany—organized into two army groups, four armies, and 61 army divisions.[8] By the end of the year, the army groups had disbanded, and two of the four armies were no longer operational. By March 1946, only one Army remained—the Third Army, which had been under the command of General George Patton during World War II, but would soon be led by General Geoffrey Keyes.[9] This rapid run-down left the Army with only three armored divisions, seven infantry divisions, and several independent regiments within nine months of the conclusion of World War II. General Dwight Eisenhower's Chief of Staff, General Walter Bedell Smith, concluded in November 1945 that "a trained, balanced force [military] . . . no longer exists."[10]

This reduction of U.S. military force corresponded to the initial demands of the postwar period. The primary goal of the military after VE Day was the redeployment of more than a million troops to Asia for the anticipated invasion of Japan. At the same time, it was felt that those who had been in the military for long periods of time, who had families at home, or who had combat experience should be eligible for demobilization. A deceptively simple point system was developed to determine who was eligible to be sent home and who would be redeployed to Japan. The result was chaotic. Brigades and regiments were classified according to the number of soldiers eligible for demobilization, but the large numbers of soldiers that Army Command shifted from unit to unit made it nearly impossible to perform any other task beyond personnel control. An Army historian of this period writes: "The field armies became little more than replacement centers. With few exceptions, critically needed persons were withdrawn without regard to the special skills required in a unit or in the theater as a whole."[11]

At the same time, the Army was expected to fan out over Germany to supervise the population in every government district—large and small. To make matters even more confusing, huge numbers of Germans, Jews, and other "displaced people" began to move to the American Zone from the East—primarily, Russia, Poland, Czechoslovakia, and Hungary. Each national group had different needs, but controlling the behavior of the Eastern refugees, especially the Poles and Jews, proved particularly troublesome.[12] One gets the impression from reading the archival records and histories of this period that the best organized Army could only have observed and reacted. But the American Army's organization was surprisingly weak shortly after accomplishing the most prestigious triumph in its history.

The combined effort to demobilize, redeploy, and establish a new occupational mission was certainly responsible for this decline in organizational capability, but this weakness may have also been due to the lack of enthusiasm of the military for its new job in Germany. Few within the Army believed that they should be responsible for the occupation government. Rather, the Army's civilian and military leadership consistently argued that occupation was a job for the State Department. Among those unwilling was George Marshall, who firmly believed that the Army should relinquish the tasks associated with occupation governance as quickly as possible.[13] High foreign policy officials in the State Department, however, were not eager for this assignment, since it did not have enough personnel for such a gargantuan task. In this case, the bureaucratic capabilities of the Army thrust it—not for the first or last time—into the reluctant position of becoming a key foreign policy actor.

This ambivalence also stemmed from uncertainty about the nature of the occupation. President Franklin Roosevelt had stated at Yalta that, "The United States would take all reasonable steps to preserve peace, but not at the expense of keeping a large army in Europe, three thousand miles away from home. The American occupation would therefore be limited to two years."[14] Most American policymakers did not believe that it would be possible to limit

European involvement to only two years. Nevertheless, Roosevelt's statement is a clear indication of the lack of any certain commitment of American troops to Europe.

In any event, the Army was forced to develop an occupation apparatus, which seemed to lead the Armed Forces even further from their traditional goal of combat readiness. On July 11, 1945, the command apparatus for the U.S. Army, SHAEF (Supreme Headquarters of Allied Expeditionary Forces), and ETOUSA (European Theater of Operations, U.S. Army), was merged into the USFET (the United States Forces, European Theater). Eisenhower remained in command of all American forces in Europe, but his headquarters moved from Rheims to the IG Farben building at Frankfurt-Hoechst. USFET became responsible for the military government in Germany's American Zone, but most of the actual administrative authority was delegated to the Deputy Military Governor, Lucius Clay, who oversaw the U.S. Group, Control Council in Berlin.

Eventually, the Third Army ceased to play any direct role in the military government in Germany. The drive to limit the Third Army's involvement in specifically German affairs stemmed from the enormous organizational confusion that plagued the beginning of German occupational government. During the combat period, the tactical army units were responsible for the rudimentary governmental activities necessary for prosecuting the war. Members of the G–5 staffs (Civil Affairs), within high- and low-level Army units, executed such tasks as traffic control, road clearing, and supply acquisition. The tactical units continued to perform these functions after VE Day, but it was now necessary to impose uniform and more complicated policies—including selecting German administrators untainted by Nazi connections—over a much larger territory.

The U.S. military had already undertaken significant planning for occupation during 1943 and 1944, but this had been necessarily separate from combat operations. Originally, the Americans and British worked together in the German Country Unit under SHAEF. During the summer after D-Day, the Allies agreed that military government planning should take place on a national level. Consequently, the work of organizing the occupational government in SHAEF gave way to that in the U.S. Group, Control Council for Germany.

The establishment of USFET during the summer of 1945 now meant that two military units ran the occupational government in the American Zone. The U.S. Group, Control Council developed the uniform policies for occupation and tried to lay the basis for the emergence of a unified Germany under four-power control, while the Civil Affairs staff (G–5) within USFET executed that policy.

In fact, the organizational flow chart was even more confusing. The two armies still active in Germany during the summer of 1945, the Seventh and Third, each had their own G–5 units, as did the corps and divisions under them. Thus, when G–5 of USFET wished to issue an order, the Chief of Staff of USFET had to be consulted before the orders could be routed to the Chiefs of Staff of the commanding generals of the Third and Seventh Armies. This cumbersome process of communication was then repeated as lower units were informed of the policy emanating from Headquarters. At each stage, the orders could be rewritten to emphasize those aspects that the particular commander preferred. To make matters worse, those charged with executing military government policies were not well integrated into the tactical units. Many of the officers (who were generally older than their colleagues in the combat units) had been trained in special schools in the United States and England and then inserted into the field. Patton's Third Army, which controlled Bavaria, was especially disdainful of the military government experts.[15]

The result of all these problems was confusion. The missteps of the early denazification efforts provide the most striking example of U.S. military disarray. During early summer 1945, "American military government detachments were operating under four different denazification directives."[16] The Third Army's policies were the most lenient, and General Patton was removed from command after stating that local Nazi officials were little different from Republicans and Democrats in the United States.[17] Patton's quip was all the more damaging because the many petty opportunists who joined the Nazis at the height of their power in Germany did resemble some of their unprincipled political colleagues to the West.

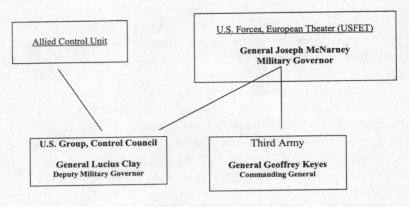

The Organization of the American Military in Occupied Germany, 1946

The Problem of GI Criminality

It is understandable that a wartime Army experiencing vast shifts in its personnel and mode of organization would have difficulty carrying out confusing and poorly articulated postwar policies. Military officials, however, prided themselves on their ability to maintain discipline even under the most chaotic circumstances. Here, the failure of Army Command to maintain authority over its soldiers was even more disturbing. The future of American policy in Europe would depend on the ability to maintain soldiers overseas. The prospects for maintaining such a policy seemed dim indeed during the immediate postwar period. The most obvious indicator of this indiscipline was the explosion of GI crime during late 1945 and early 1946.

It is difficult to get an accurate picture of crime committed by GIs in Germany. The categories used by the Provost Marshal's office of the Third Army varied, and it was not always easy to make sure that "serious incidents" were recorded in the same way. Still, the data from the monthly historical reports are revealing and, to my knowledge, have not been analyzed systematically.

During the first ten months of the occupation—between May 1945 and March 1946—the Provost Marshal's office of the Third Army listed the "serious incidents" that were reported and assigned for investigation. Deeds subject to this classification were criminal

The Complex Communication of Occupation Policy in the U.S. Military, Summer 1945

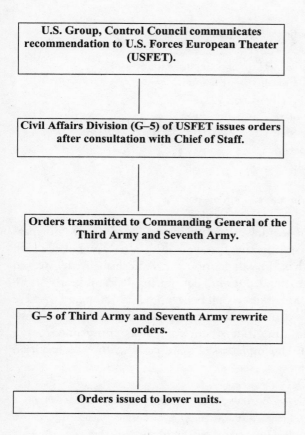

acts of violence and theft. For example, the October 1945 "Historical Report" included:

1. Larceny—six incidents
2. Rape—five
3. Pilferage—two
4. Accidental shooting—one
5. Theft—two

6. Injury (shooting)–one
7. Suicide (shooting)–one
8. Assault–one
9. Murder–three
10. Misappropriation of government property–three
11. Black marketing–three
12. Possession of American and English money–one
13. Assault with a deadly weapon–two
14. Assault and battery (robbery)–one
15. Alleged sale of poison liquor–two
16. Alleged rape–one
17. Manslaughter–one
18. Rape (Assault)–one
19. Larceny and assault–one
20. Assault with intent to murder–one[18]

The grand total of serious incidents was 42—a relatively "normal" monthly amount during the first year after VE Day, but a much higher number than the contemporary American Army would accept. (The occupation troops in Haiti during 1995 and early 1996, for example, were remarkably well behaved when compared to these data.) Moreover, as demobilization proceeded, the evidence suggests that the crime *rate* rose. Indeed, commentators complained of an epidemic of crime during late 1945 and early 1946.[19] As historian Earl Ziemke notes:

> To add to the strain on the unsettled and unhappy country, violence of all kinds, excepting resistance to the occupation authorities, increased in the early half of 1946. Incidents caused by U.S. troops, if no more numerous than they had been in last months of 1945, were certainly no fewer; they included as they had earlier, wanton killing, looting, and threats and assaults on German police and civilians.[20]

The high crime rate continued into the second year of the occupation. The figures reported by the Provost Marshal's office suggest a murder rate *higher* than existed in the District of Columbia during the mid-1990s—when this troubled city was known as the murder capital of the U.S. If the Army had numbered 600,000—approximately the size of D.C.'s population—the number of murders committed would have been 492 during a nine-month period.[21] During all of 1994, Washington suffered 399 homicides.

How are we to understand the high and even rising crime rate of the early occupation years? It should be noted that a comparison of an Army of young men—the most crime-prone population within human society—with a city of all different ages is problematic. One would expect large groups of young men to exhibit more violent, antisocial behavior. On the other hand, the Army is a disciplined and hierarchical organization largely because the military is comprised of young men. Officers impose strict discipline in order to channel the comparative advantage in violence that the Army's demographic composition offers. Normally, strict, routinized discipline does successfully constrain the behavior of soldiers. The criminal behavior of the Army in Germany between 1945 and 1947 was not normal.

The Economic Roots of GI Criminality

> Send the money home instead. The things you really need . . . are always available at the Post Exchange . . . Keep your clothing and equipment in shape, and most of all–KEEP IT! Selling food and clothing on the black market is a way of profiting directly from the war-born misery and poverty of the European peoples. . . . Selling government property is another way to get a stiff court martial sentence entered on your service record.[22]

There is little doubt that black marketing activity was on the mind of occupation soldiers and their officers. After all, the opportunities were immense. Not only were German civilians hungry for goods and an effective medium of exchange, but American policy either purposefully or inadvertently gave soldiers an enormous incentive to loot their own stores and market supplies to the diverse civilian and martial populations living in Germany after World War II.

During the war, the United States and the other Allies in Europe had to determine how to manage the currencies of conquered territories. There was a general consensus that the dollar should not be introduced into Europe as a medium of exchange, since its presence would make it much more difficult for an indigenous government to reintroduce a stable domestic currency. At the same time, the invading armies needed to be able to command local resources efficiently as military units pushed back the Nazis and established a more permanent hold over newly liberated territories.

The solution was to issue Allied military currencies (marks, francs, yen, etc.) which would be exchanged at par with domestic monies. American soldiers in the field were paid in this currency, but could trade in their military francs, lira, or marks for dollars at a predetermined rate. This attempt to preserve the value of wages paid to soldiers permitted GIs to sell goods from U.S. military stores to the domestic population in return for the local currency. It was then possible to exchange the currency for dollars and send the profits home.

The potential for profits in Germany was particularly great. The fixed rate set by the Army allowed soldiers to convert ten Reich marks for one dollar, even though in May 1945, the street rate of exchange was 200 Reich marks for one dollar.[23] Julian Bach, Jr., an associate editor of *Life* magazine, suggests, in one of the first book-length journalistic accounts of the occupation, that a mildly enterprising soldier would have been able to exploit this enormous difference by purchasing cigarettes, candy, and liquor from the PX stores and reselling the items to impoverished customers outside the American compound. If done systematically, such a soldier could acquire a gross annual income of $11,820 at a cost of $93.20.[24] Many soldiers masked their "arbitrage" activities by reporting enormous gambling winnings, since only a perfunctory oath was necessary to account for the cash surplus a GI might acquire.[25]

The sellers of goods were able to rely on a very generous distribution system that made the Army personnel the most pampered of the occupation armies. Franklin Davis recalls: "In Germany, the post exchanges sprang forth as great bastions of plenty in the midst of poverty—in Frankfurt, a special building was put up, in Wiesbaden a downtown department store was taken over, in Heidelberg a huge warehouse was renovated. . . . And there was more liquor than a man could drink."[26]

The major source of demand for PX goods came from Germans

and "Displaced Persons." The impoverished population of the occupation zone desired food, clothing, and a medium of exchange such
as cigarettes and (to a lesser extent) candy. Reich marks carried little purchasing power, and paid jobs were often only sought in order
to obtain a food ration book.[27] On the other hand, cigarettes were
storable, portable and divisible: all key characteristics for any money.
A whole cigarette collection industry developed that employed German children. Waiters in restaurants and clubs, which GIs fre-
quented, were especially prized occupations. Bach reports that an
anonymous study found no cigarette butt remained in an ashtray for
more than 45 seconds in Kurfuerstendamm cafes in Berlin.[28]

These economic conditions applied to all of Germany, but black
marketing pressures were particularly intense in Berlin. Unlike the
American military personnel, the Russian could not convert their
marks into rubles. All Allied military mark pay had to be spent in
Germany, and the Russians were inevitably drawn to the American
soldiers wherever they were in close proximity. For this reason, illegal trading was particularly intense between American and Soviet
soldiers. Red Army personnel could use the Allied military marks
printed in their zone to purchase American goods—watches were
especially prized—and the GIs could then convert the marks into
dollars. Indeed, Bach refers to the new meaning of "the Watch on
the Rhine" in the following account:

> "A run-of-the-factory watch brings between $200 and $600. A watch with
> several dials, a black face and red second hand, brings $1300. It makes no dif-
> ference what any of these watches originally cost. . . . The Russians think
> the Americans are crazy to part with their watches, and the Americans think
> the Russians are crazy to part with so much money for a watch."[29]

During July 1945, Americans in Berlin sent home four times as
many dollars as they were paid. (The payroll was $1 million and they
sent home $4 million.) Despite the greater presence of Russians, this
problem was not limited to Berlin. During October 1945, $36 mil-
lion "extra" dollars left the European Theater.[30] It is important to
note that black market operations instigated by American troops
became a chronic problem for all American occupation govern-

ments. As Andrew Overby, Special Assistant to the Secretary of the Treasury, noted before the June 1947 Congressional hearings: "The problem existed in other areas, and in one of the Western European countries in relation to the troops, it was, in my judgment, equal in proportion to the German problem."[31]

The fact that illegal currency trading was an epidemic throughout Europe did not lessen the problem. Indeed, officers were often sympathetic to the soldiers' acquisitive drive because of Germany's status as a defeated enemy. General Lucien Truscott, one-time commander of the Third Army, explained clearly the general problem of imposing economic restrictions on soldiers:

> The soldier felt that he and his buddy had won the war, and they wanted nothing so much as return to normal civil life. He had demonstrated his willingness and ability to submit to controls essential for winning the war. He had demonstrated that he was the finest soldier of all time. But these men were still American, with the American characteristic of resenting controls and restrictions that they considered an interference with individual rights and liberties. The soldier could see no reason why he should not sell personal items which he had purchased, or which had been sent to him from home, if he so desired. After all, he believed in democracy and individual human rights and in our system of free enterprise for which he had fought. Letters from home, newspapers, and radios informed him that many at home who had not suffered his hardships were making profits from the war, as he felt, at his expense. He could see no reason why he should not make a small profit now when he had for the first time a small opportunity to do so. He considered that transmitting money home was an individual right and a small recompense for his sacrifice.[32]

The clear sympathy for GI grievances (real or imaginary—many of the soldiers in Germany by 1946 had not suffered through combat) may explain the Army's reluctance to devise obvious changes in its currency policy to stop black marketing activity. One effect of this dilatory response was that the incentive to steal German or American assets was that much greater.

Requisitioning and Theft

During the occupation period itself, most media accounts of economic crimes focused on the spectacular cases—the most famous being the theft of the Hessian crown jewels by two American officers. The crime involved royalty, sex, and malfeasance among those in command—a perfect combination for *Current Affairs*. (We can only imagine how contemporary television would have covered the occupation of Germany.)

In this case, WAC Captain Kathleen Nash took jewels that were found in the wine cellar of Kronberg castle, which GIs had invaded shortly before VE Day. At the time, she told the family of the Hessian prince and princess (who was Kaiser Wilhelm's sister and Queen Victoria's granddaughter) that the U.S. Army would take custody of the jewels. Unfortunately, when Captain Nash married Colonel J.S. Durant and they demobilized together, the jewels wound up in their possession in Chicago. The Hessian royal family complained, and the larcenous couple was returned to Germany for trial.[33]

This incident was perhaps the most widely publicized crime committed by American officers, but not really the cleverest. My favorite evokes the criminal misdeeds of an early Alec Guiness film. The headline on page seven of the January 5, 1946 edition of the *New York Times* reads "GI Gang Seized in Boxcar. Directed Freight Robberies from Swank Rail Hideout in Germany." Datelined Herford, Germany, I include the full article:

> Six AWOL American soldiers were arrested January 1, it was announced today, in a luxuriously furnished boxcar from which they allegedly had conducted large-scale train robberies and black market operations during the last eighteen months.
>
> British troops led by American officers caught four of the gang as they reclined on easy chairs with German girls. The others were seized when they returned in a jeep.
>
> The six posed as American security police, an official said, and induced real transport officers in the British and American zones of Germany to arrange the coupling of food cars on trains. The loaded cars were later dropped off on sidings and the contents sold, it was said.[34]

These accounts suggest that all property was fair game for the criminal elements in the American army. Indeed, the records indicate significant amounts of looting of American as well as German property. The theft of American assets was particularly severe during the first year after VE Day. Large numbers of soldiers only loosely attached to disorganized units made it possible for the enterprising to acquire jewels, live in a "swank" boxcar, or raid liquor stocks. Moreover, the huge amount of supplies remaining from the war effort as well as the disrepair of the German rail system made looting and black marketing very attractive. Oliver Frederiksen reports that during December 1945, $2 million of American stocks disappeared, which represented 2 percent of the 11 million tons of supplies in the European Theater.[35] According to Frederiksen, the rate of "disappearance" declined throughout 1946, but that supplies were not really secure until German industrial police were assigned to guard installations during the summer of 1947.[36]

The German Thieving Field

The reliance on German police to secure American property from American soldiers is ironic on so many levels that it is perhaps best not to comment. Still, it is necessary to underline one point: the real tensions associated with economic misdeeds centered on the status of German property. The problems began with the invasion of Germany. Two stories indicate that Germany became a thieving field for enlisted men and officers alike during the combat and immediate post combat period. John Gimbel reports that when the Army entered Marburg: "The Combat troops who entered the city took watches, cameras, radios, and furniture promiscuously."[37]

An anecdote told by Calvin Hoover, one of the chief economic advisors to Lucius Clay in Berlin, is even more revealing:

> There was no question of "a correct attitude towards a defeated foe." On our way up from Versailles, a captain, a graduate of my own university [Duke], now an administrative officer in the 8th Air Force, boasted that he and some of his pals had taken off from England into our occupation area in a Flying Fortress immediately after the German surrender. They had put down at a

former German airfield and had unloaded a jeep that they had brought with them. They then ranged about the countryside, looting cameras, radios, and anything else that took their fancy. They then flew to an airfield in France and peddled their loot on the black market.[38]

The occupation period, however, was meant to be different. A chief premise of the American occupation was that the rule of law would be established, which both occupiers and occupied would follow. Commitments to legal process were fundamental to the effort to denazify and democratize German society. It might be excusable for soldiers, flushed with victory over a repugnant political system, to take advantage of their power.[39] It was not acceptable, however, for the occupation government to create a climate that encouraged American lawlessness.

That the criminal theft of German property was not unusual well into the occupation is demonstrated by the following 1946 incident, reported by Earl Ziemke: "An enlisted man in the detachment [of Laufen, Bavaria] had held up the local post office for 35,0000 marks. When asked why the theft had not been reported, the postmaster said the soldier had threatened to have him thrown in jail if he did and the general behavior of the detachment was such that he believed the threat."[40]

The problem that the Army faced in imposing discipline did not just stem from a failure to identify the minority of soldiers who were prone to take without asking. Taking without asking or requisitioning was basic to the governance of the American occupation. When Captain Nash took the Hessian Crown Jewels, she was acting as if she were requisitioning them along with the rest of the property of Kronberg castle. The gap between seizing for temporary use and stealing was often not large.

Hoover again writes vividly about this problem:

In the early days of our occupation, almost anyone could requisition almost anything from the German population. If the owner were lucky, he might be able to obtain a signed form from the requisitioning officer, which theoretically would entitle him to some form of compensation from some as yet unknown governmental authority. However, cases came to my attention where requisitions had been signed "Captain Mickey Mouse" or "Major Napoleon Bonapart" or simply "Captain Yur Stuk." Sometimes a lieutenant in one of the engineering battalions would take over construction equipment from some German construction company, and when he had no further use for it would simply abandon it in a wood fifty miles away. Substantially all automobiles belonging to German civilians were taken over by our troops, usually for some more or less official use. Bicycles were sometimes simply seized by our GIs. This process of informally seizing property had begun when our troops took over occupied areas in Italy, France, or other countries after expelling the German troops. Then all property that the Germans had previously requisitioned from the native population was fair game for our troops. The process of taking over automobiles was known as "liberating." This term continued to be used when our troops liberated German-owned automobiles. It was even extended so that it became customary of the GI's to speak of "liberating a blonde."[41]

Nor was this a matter of enlisted men's misbehavior. Many of the complaints centered on the rapaciousness of high-ranking officers. Robert Murphy, the State Department's designated political advisor to Clay, tells the following story:

Even some high-ranking Americans developed peculiar twists in their attitude toward German possessions. I remember in particular one officer whom I invited to dinner soon after I was settled in Berlin. American troops in Germany were quartered in tents, Quonset huts, and other barrack constructions, but German residences had been commandeered for most of our officers and civilian staffs. I was lucky enough to have assigned to me a pleasant but unpretentious house with a small garden. Among the furnishings was an upholstered chair that my officer guest found agreeably comfortable. After longing in it for an hour after dinner, he said to me, "The chairs in my house are too stiff. I need this chair to put next to my reading lamp." I thought he was merely making conversation, so I smiled amiably. But the next day his aide appeared at my residence, saying that his superior had instructed him to collect the upholstered chair. I sent the aide away empty-handed, with a verbal message for his chief that probably was toned down before delivery. To be sure, the requisitioned furniture in my official residence did not belong to me, but neither did it belong to my appreciative guest.[42]

Most histories of the occupation government also suggest that officers experienced enormous difficulty in wresting property from tactical units as the size of their units declined. General Lucius Clay himself comments that: "We had to establish military government units, take over from the tactical troops. The tactical troops did not want to give up, because as long as they were in charge they could commandeer houses, and whatever they wanted, and they liked that sense of power."[43]

There was much to return to German property owners. By the end of June 1946, the Army had requisitioned the following properties:

24,502 private homes
1,458 apartment houses
780 schools
333 office buildings
263 factory buildings
222 warehouses and depots
103 retail stores
457 pieces of land
1,279 properties of other types[44]

The early reasons for requisitioning were clear. In the first place, seizing property, especially from Nazi sympathizers, was one definitive way to impose occupation costs directly on the German population *and* punish them for their association with the Hitler regime. As long as occupation authorities subscribed to the theory of collective guilt, there was no reason for Americans to be unduly worried about possibly enjoying the fruits of victory illegitimately. Still, one can sense the unease in Julian Bach's description of one requisitioned house. "The house to which we drove, and in which my host and his 22 men live, contains 25 rooms. The roof and third floor are damaged, but, unlike most houses in the neighborhood, the lower floors are intact. . . . The owner, widow of a former German consular official, now lives down the block with friends in an unheated house with cardboards in the window."[45]

Moreover, this unease often turned to disquiet and, in some cases, disgust, when eyewitnesses described the uglier reality of American requisitioning.[46] Given the less than sterling patterns of behavior by American soldiers and the need to rely on Germans for governance, the theory of collective guilt could not be applied indefinitely to Germans any more than the Union Army could apply it to the white southern population of the occupied South after the Civil War. (Many Germans noted with some justification that the racist persecution of blacks linked white Americans closer to Germans than many Americans would like to admit.)

The American drive for comfort and ease at German expense could not be justified for long. A working partnership required that American behavior be somehow restrained. It would no longer be acceptable for troops to hunt "at night with spotlights and [to fish] with hand grenades."[47] Nor could "blondes be liberated" or citizens removed from their houses at two hours' notice. After the first year of occupation, a new culture governing relations between occupiers and occupied would have to be found. At the center of this restructuring would have to be a greater respect for German and American property from the average GI Joe.

Chapter II

"Primarily Interested in the German Fraulein"[1]

Sexual Activity and Crime

Sexual activity was central to the American experience with Germans during the first years of the occupation. Sex caused more headaches for Army Command than any other "illicit" GI behavior. Because of the sensitivity of this issue for the American and German populations alike, the routinization of intimacy was central to the stabilization of the Army's presence in Germany. Normalizing sex amounted to discovering which relations between American men and German women would be acceptable—not just to Army Command but also to young German men, young American women and the mothers and fathers of both lands. In short, the Army's search for politically correct sexual relations tells us much about the social relations that the occupation helped to establish between the American and German people.

Many of the violent crimes committed by soldiers—particularly assaults and rapes—stemmed from the problematic nature of the sexual relations being established between young German women and young American men. Most histories of the occupation government complain that military government officers spent much of their time attempting to limit the damage that GI misbehavior did to the governing mission of the occupation authority. The worst events invariably occurred near midnight on weekends. Then, excessive drinking combined with sexual competition led to numerous clashes among American troops as well as between American and German men.

Each quarterly report summarizing the Third Army's activities beginning January 1, 1946, stressed the tense relations existing between German and American men. At first, the emphasis was on the violent behavior of American troops. "Unprovoked attacks by United States personnel on German civilians in Munich, Nuremberg, and Dachau, fostered an animosity that indirectly provoked the worst elements of the civil populace to action. A concurrent rise was noticed in the number of incidents involving American colored troops. The entire situation is conducive to future trouble. . . ."[2]

The following chapter details the racial animosity that plagued the Third Army. However, race played only an exacerbating role in heightening the tensions associated with what the Army called "fraternization"—that is, the establishment of intimate relations between members of the occupation Army and German women. In mid-1946, the Third Army reported:

Fraternization, with all of its various implications and ramifications, has come to be an accepted part of the occupation of Germany and the only time the subject assumes importance any more is usually in connection with crimes that disturb internal security. During January sixteen attacks were made on United States military personnel. These assaults were carried on for the most part by small groups of German male civilians as an expression of their dislike for fraternization on the part of German girls. The records of February and March also reveal that a substantial number of the cases of attacks on United States military personnel were prompted by this urge of young German males to stop the association of German girls with United States soldiers.[3]

(All of the older texts and documents refer to women as *girls* or *frauleins*. I reproduce the language in these articles without employing *sic* after every sexist phrase.)

It is doubtful that German attacks on Americans equaled the number of assaults on Germans by American soldiers. The Third Army Command, however, was concerned that the animosity bred by sexual relations might undermine the occupation and give birth to a new Fascist movement. For this reason, the authors of the Army's historical reports attempted to link German male animosity toward the GI to the small incidents of pro-Hitler sabotage. The proof of such an actual linkage in German political life was scanty, but the Army's reports tried to establish a connection simply by placing descriptions of serious criminal incidents connected to sexual competition next to discussions of rather trivial efforts by a small number of Germans to support Nazism. "In Munich on 5 July an American soldier and a German girl were found shot and killed in a vacant lot. Two instances of decapitating wires were noted in the same month, and Nazi flags, swastikas, and arms in the possession of Germans were discovered."[4]

The implausibility of the regular Army's campaign attempt to link the rebirth of Nazism to the tensions associated with German–American sexual relations should not lead us to dismiss the problem caused by German–American sexual contact. The Army could not comfortably tolerate an environment in which there was a "substantial number of attacks on United States military personnel in the company of German girls . . . by individuals or small groups of German male civilians as an expression of their dislike for the association of German girls with United States soldiers."[5] Nor could the occasional murder of an American by a German male sit well with Army Command. "A soldier, spending the night with his girl friend in Stuttgart, was shot and killed by the girl's estranged husband who surprised them in the morning."[6]

Unfortunately, it was difficult to find a solution to the tensions caused by heterosexually active American males and German females. Moreover, Army attempts to regulate the sexual activity of soldiers began on an extraordinarily inauspicious note.

The Fraternization Ban Disaster

This story begins with the fraternization ban. At the close of the war and during the first few months of the occupation, the Army attempted to enforce a complete ban on communication between Germans and Americans. The prohibition on communication was so severe that it was not even clear that military government detachments could establish communication with those Germans charged with carrying out occupation policy. The core of the problem, however, was that GIs treated the regulation with contempt.

Some of the jokes told by GIs indicate the source of this resistance to Army Command.

> The German soldiers [are] getting a discharge, donning civilian clothes, and making love to the women while they [the U.S. troops] are the ones virtually in prison. . . . The policy is just to give the brass the first crack at all the good-looking women.[7]

The soldiers saw themselves in competition with other men for sexual access to German women, and perceived any measure to reduce their freedom of action as inherently unfair.

The failure of the fraternization ban was evident to all—almost from the moment American troops entered German soil. Such a policy could only have been enforced by the use of extremely harsh measures. As Harold Zink notes: "Despite all of the military police who roamed the countryside in jeeps to enforce the non-fraternization ban [*sic*], it became increasingly apparent that the American Army would have to give itself to court martialing on an enormous scale and construct gigantic stockades to house the offenders; or wink at what was going on, thus jeopardizing any degree of discipline and order or modify the non-fraternization ban."[8]

Given the not very (or, perhaps, all too) edifying spectacle of a conquering Army unable to impose its will on its own troops, the fraternization ban quickly unraveled. On June 8, 1945, Dwight Eisenhower declared that non-fraternization did not apply to children.[9] Two months later, members of the Army Command were permitted to have "normal" contacts with the subject population. Finally, on October 1, the Allied Control Council ratified reality and removed all restrictions on relations with Germans with two exceptions. Germans could not live in houses that billeted troops, and marriage between occupation forces and Germans was still prohibited. (The first exception had the unintended effect of perpetuating the harsh manner of requisitioning which characterized the early months of the occupation.) The marriage ban was not particularly effective, since surreptitiously performed marriages before a recognized religious authority were considered legal and "gave the wife the right to immigrate to the United States on a non-quota basis, full rights to allotments from the soldier's pay and from government funds, and transportation to the United States at government expense as a war bride."[10]

Toward the end of 1946, the Army announced that marriage would be permitted during the last month of duty. By June 1948, Americans and Germans had contracted 3,500 legal marriages.[11]

Rampant Fraternization

As Harold Zink's comments suggest, there is little indication that the fraternization ban inhibited the GIs in their pursuit of women. John Gimbel reports that the first troops to enter Marburg "opened the doors of the prisons and released criminals as well as political prisoners. They were kind to children and friendly with women, but hostile toward men. They apparently respected the non-fraternization regulations only in their dealings with men."[12]

A few months later, the word *fraternization* entered into the ordinary lexicon of postwar American life. In fact, *Life* magazine obliquely suggested in one of its first reports on the American–German heterosexual activity that the word *fraternization* had replaced the better-known *f*-word to designate the search for sexual intercourse. Julian Bach notes that when a soldier was going out, he often proclaimed: "I'm going frattin."[13]

The scale of fraternization is more difficult to estimate. There seems to be a general consensus that American soldiers were the most active chasers of German women after battle conditions stabilized. Russian soldiers were feared because of the mass rapes that occurred during the invasion, but after the Soviet Army decided to discourage rape, the Russian soldiers did not have the economic resources to compete with Americans for German women. The British soldiers also seemed to exhibit more self-control. For example, Alec Cairncross proudly comments, "Here and elsewhere I heard the conduct of the British soldier contrasted favorably with that of the American GI in dealings with women and property. The

British troops in Berlin had in fact a remarkably high discipline, and a quite impressive bearing, generally intelligent and humane."[14] Most American commentators were not willing to grant the moral superiority of the "Limey." Still, Bach does admit that the relative extent of British fraternization was about half that of the typical American unit.[15]

David Reynolds' excellent work *Rich Relations* provides some explanations for this difference. Reynolds argues that George Marshall had attempted to mold an American Army of draftees by combining traditional discipline with new services intended to promote the soldiers' material welfare. Efforts to keep PXs well-stocked and to offer wide-ranging entertainment programs raised morale but created enormous material divisions between "wealthy" American soldiers and impoverished European populations. With this wealth came the power of young men to command all kinds of personal services from those much less affluent.[16]

Most of these accounts are impressionistic, but the Army did also survey its troops on this question during the fall of 1945. The results are revealing. According to this survey, about 56 percent of the soldiers had spent some time "talking" with German "girls" during the week of the interview. Twenty-five percent "talked" for ten hours or more per week. It is not clear from the report on this survey whether the conversation between largely monolingual German speakers and largely monolingual English speakers was with one or more than one woman. In any event, the report clearly suggests that during any given week, more than one-quarter of the troops were having some form of sex with German women.[17] (The survey indicates that very few American soldiers had any contact with German men of their age. Many of them were still in prison and work camps in the Soviet Union. Thus, the possibility of forming homosexual attachments between American and German men was quite limited.)

Fraternization as a Public Health Problem: The Attempt to Control Venereal Disease

The scale of German–American sexual activity had a large number of repercussions for the American occupation authorities, but the major issue that Army Command focused on throughout the early occupation was venereal disease (VD). The problem was truly staggering. Oliver J. Frederiksen reports that VD rates among soldiers rose 235 percent between VE Day and the end of 1945—from 75 per 1,000 soldiers per year to 251 per 1,000 soldiers per year. The weekly reports on this problem are not always recorded in the Third Army's monthly or quarterly "Histories." Nevertheless, enough data exist from June 1946 through January 1947 to indicate that VD contraction remained at this very high level for almost a year. This latter figure does not mean that one-fourth of the troops had contracted venereal disease. Rather, it suggests that, if the weekly rate of detection remained constant for the whole year, the number of annual VD cases would be equivalent to one-quarter of the Army. Thus, if somewhat less than five cases were uncovered every week within a hypothetical Army unit of 1,000, this would be equivalent to an annual rate of 250 per 1,000. Of course, this method of calculation counts repeat "offenders."[18]

Some commentators have blamed this increase in VD on the replacement troops. Frederiksen, for instance, claims that, "There were many reasons for this increase, including the relative youth and immaturity of the postwar replacements, the great numbers of infected women in Europe after the war, the desperate economic situation leading to prostitution, and poor morale and discipline among the troops. The too easy availability of alcoholic beverages and the faith of the troops in the curative powers of penicillin were contributing factors."[19]

Of all the explanations listed here, the focus on the replacement troops is probably the least compelling. Contemporary accounts suggest that a high percentage of combat veterans participated eagerly in the search of sexually available women.[20] (The rape figures discussed in the preceding chapter suggest that soldiers did not always ascertain the willingness of women to engage in sex.) On the other hand, there is no doubt that poverty and organizational confusion were major reasons for prostitution and the spread of VD. "The fundamental source of the epidemic . . . was the poverty of the Germans that made sex easy to obtain, as well as the confusion and upheaval that attended the organizational changes in the theater

Table 2.1   Venereal Disease Rates (per 1,000 per year) in the Third Army   (June 1946–January 1947)

Date	White	Black	Combined
6/15/46	156	827	240
6/22/46	157	646	220
6/29/46	160	971	246
7/13/46	153	626	229
8/10/46	189	744	255
8/17/46	142	522	188
8/24/46	178	600	227
8/31/46		944	255
9/7/46		643	208
9/14/46			182
9/21/46			179
9/28/46	119	777	192
10/5/46	131	646	184
10/12/46			186
10/19/46			171
10/26/46			130
11/2/46	126	458	168
11/16/46	134	522	176
11/30/46			162
12/28/46	108	349	130
1/4/47		228	118
1/18/47		468	149

Source: Headquarters, Third U.S. Army, Chief of Staff Section, "Report of Operations" (Quarterly) and "History of the Command Section, Third Army" (Monthly) (Suitland, MD: National Archives, Record Group 338, Boxes 66 and 67.) For a more complete explanation of the term *rate* see the preceding paragraph.

and the dispatch of troops to the Pacific or to home. . . . Control of venereal disease had always depended upon command responsibility. For the moment lines of authority were hopelessly confused. . . ."[21]

VD was not just a public health problem, but it was convenient for Army Command to treat it as such. The limitation of the illness would create fewer problems for the folks back home—who certainly did not want their sons to return tainted or "burned." Moreover, the new German authorities had a clear interest in regulating VD in such a way that the American Army's presence would prove to be less disruptive. Finally, actual attempts to control VD seemed to work better if authorities "medicalized" the problem.

The first loosening of the ban on fraternization in early June 1945 included the decision that the presence of a venereal infection would not be grounds for discipline. This encouraged soldiers to receive treatment and permitted the Army to intensify the aggressive distribution of "V–Packettes" to all soldiers and establish prophylactic stations at Red Cross Clubs and train stations throughout the occupied territories.[22] The V–Packettes included condoms and chemical prophylactics. Normally, soldiers could receive more supplies without difficulty, and units also provided pamphlets and held lectures on VD prevention. The key to all these treatment programs was the liberal use of penicillin to control the disease. This medical intervention only came into use during the war and strongly supported the Army's relatively amoral efforts to control the epidemic.[23]

The most contentious issue concerned the regulation of prostitution and, more generally, women's bodies. The Army's official policy was to repress prostitution and aggressively trace female carriers of disease. This latter control mechanism seemed to be employed by all units in cooperation with the largely male German political leaders. On the other hand, some officers believed that it was useful to sponsor houses of prostitution where soldiers were massed. Post–D-Day France was the major territory in which such measures were implemented. One officer charged with coordinating public health policy "found in Cherbourg 'houses of prostitution being run for, and indirectly by, U.S. troops.' One establishment had been designated for black soldiers, the others for whites, and military police [were] stationed at the doors to keep order in the queues that formed."[24]

Such sponsorship of prostitution evidently did not exist in Germany, but this did not mean that Army officers did not attempt to influence the pattern of sexual relations between American men and German women. In Weilburg, Hesse, Captain Arthur Volz, the senior Liaison and Security Officer of his military government detachment, decided to permit those who had relationships with soldiers of an

Army unit to settle in Weilburg if the unit moved into the territory—even though this policy was against Army regulations.

The reason for this was to encourage sexual relations of relatively
long standing and discourage "chance contacts," Volz explains:

> To find out just how many new people came into the area with or after a
> new unit, it was made known that they should report to the Liaison and
> Security Office. Here they were registered, along with the full data on the
> soldier sponsoring them. They were screened and on approval were given
> temporary local identification papers and directed to the German authori-
> ties for quarters. In this way all established relationships were discovered,
> controlled and watched. Through German police and informants, and Liai-
> son and Security checks, tab was kept on the girls and soldiers. If any trou-
> ble resulted the girl was expelled from the *Kreis,* losing her billet and papers.
> As a result we had little if any trouble with this group. In some cases we were
> actually able to provided [*sic*] assistance in cases of genuine need.[25]

At the same time, the Liaison and Security Office carried out a vigorous campaign against prostitution that led to the expulsion of all
women who could not be locally identified. Finally, "raids were
made on places in town and in the woods around the Kaserne. The
latter proved to be the greatest source of VD. Here women maintained tent camps under most filthy conditions. Repeat offenders,
with or without VD, were given jail sentences. In this way the major
source of VD was wiped out."[26]

Similar techniques were probably used by other military government detachments, but there were risks. The borderline legality of
this VD control activity (which was predicated on the assumption
that "the VD problem was one of public health, not of morals")[27]
made a military government detachment vulnerable to official complaints. Volz reports, for example, that one battalion commander
who "had given very strict orders against the movement of civilians
into Weilburg" nevertheless registered several women himself. When
he tried to force the Liaison and Security Office to provide him
with unwarranted housing, he attempted to blackmail the Military
Government officers by revealing their unorthodox VD control policy to higher authorities. Volz responded by noting that he had lists

of the women he had registered for residence in the town. The Lieutenant Colonel never did receive the housing he requested.

It is important to note that this small Liaison and Security Office may have had more autonomy than others because all four members of it could speak German. Thus, it was not necessary to rely on interpreters to track the activity of the subject population. On the other hand, all tactical and Liaison and Security units were under considerable pressure to do something about venereal disease. The most obvious technique was to regulate the nature of the cross-national male-female contact.

Thus, most military officers did attempt to introduce measures that would encourage soldiers to have relationships with "clean" women. One technique that did not work well was the attempt to sponsor women as suitable to attend troop entertainment. Ziemke sardonically comments, "Quite a few [army units] experimented with systems of social passes. The passes were issued to girls of presumed good character and admitted them to unit events. Unfortunately, some implications of being registered made it difficult to interest the kinds of girls commands wanted most."[28] By November 1946, the European Command abandoned the attempt to have registered women submit to physical examinations.[29]

Power, Sex, and Politics in Occupied Germany

The high rate of sexual activity within the American Army in Germany represented more than a public health problem or crime problem. The exercise of power was inevitably at the core of almost every sexual contact between Germans and Americans, and this reality made sex political in the sense that the stabilization of intimate relations between conqueror and conquered went hand-in-hand with the establishment of "normalized" German–American relations.

Cynthia Enloe perceptively explains how sex gets linked to these "grander" political issues:

> Understanding how a military base acquires its local camouflage—or perhaps loses it—is critical to making sense of how international military alliances are perpetuated, or undone. The normalcy that sustains a military base in a

local community rests on ideas about masculinity and femininity. A foreign base requires especially delicate adjustment of relations between men and women, for if the fit between local and foreign men and local and foreign women breaks down, the base may lose its protective cover. It may become the target of nationalist resentment that could subvert the very structure of a military alliance.[30]

The behavior of many American soldiers certainly exacerbated German–American tensions. In a book published in 1947, Andy Rooney—a former *Stars and Stripes* reporter and recent *60 Minutes* commentator—and co-author, Bud Hutton, note, "Americans have behaved as it never would have occurred to them to behave at home. . . . In itself, it is a comic and unimportant example, but at one time General McNarney had to use the dignity and power of a four-star general to stop the American soldier's habit of leaning out of a moving jeep to slap the fannies of frauleins walking along the sidewalk or along the roadside where rubble covered the walks. Fanny slapping got to be the Great American Game for a short month before it was stopped by a strongly worded official head-quarters communiqué."[31]

The period of rampant fraternization during the early occupation highlights the dangers of nationalist reaction very well. German males were in little position to protest American sexual abuses effectively, but there is no doubt that many males resented American attempts to monopolize "their" women. Bach reports an extreme example of this anger when he translates a poster put up around Berlin during the early occupation period.

What German women and girls do,
Makes a man weep, not laugh.
One bar of chocolate or one piece of gum
Gives her the name German whore. . . .
When such a woman should desire a German husband,
She should go to hell.
The devil does not want such creatures and will
Throw them on the dung, thinking,
"Dirt belongs to dirt."[32]

American authorities controlled these reactions and related reports of German women getting their heads shaved by male youth relatively easily. U.S. power could effectively crush any German male resistance to fraternization. The problem was not in physical suppression, but in developing a new interpretive framework that would lead the German male to work cooperatively with American male authority. Julian Bach, for example, argues that a key test of the German male's readiness to discard his Nazi past was his ability to accept the reality of American male–German female heterosexual relations. "There is more at stake here than the mere question of how Germans react to the sight of Americans with German girls. . . . The extent to which German men accept 'fratting' is the thermometer that registers the degree to which they accept defeat, contain their national pride and look forward to a new and more congenial way of life. Obviously the sight of a German woman with an American conqueror enrages an unreconstructed German more than a German who is anxious to cooperate with us."[33] In other words, the ability of the German male to recognize and accept the individual rights of German women and American men to pursue sex with whomever they want revealed his ability to work within a democratic political framework.

Such assertions of individual liberty are superficially plausible, but neglect the underlying coercive conditions that informed the "free choice" of sexual partners in Germany. As late as 1949, the German police were still having difficulty controlling drunken GIs in pursuit of young women. Police Chief Drzmilla of Augsburg comments that, after the rule prohibiting Americans from visiting German taverns was temporarily lifted, "Most Americans behaved themselves, [but] there were fights, because of girls and drunkenness, in which the German usually was helpless and was thoroughly beaten up."[34]

A former soldier just back from Germany perhaps best described those conditions for the GI in Germany that permitted the successful pursuit of sex with women. "At the risk of letting the cat out of the bag, it must be admitted that all the GI wants in Europe is a "good deal"—that is a comfortable place to sleep, food at all times, a woman to [do] laundry and pressing for cigarettes or candy, no Army duty requiring labor, and a chance to fraternize as often as possible. . . . In Germany, naturally, the GI finds the best deal. . . . In France the deal is different. The GI doesn't find the all-out bootlicking of Germany. He can't make France the plaything he heard it was from his Dad and from the liberators of 1944."[35]

Given this freedom, the American soldiers in Germany often seemed to exhibit no self-control at all. In Marburg, for example, "The dean of the theological faculty reported that he escaped serious injury at the hands of irresponsible soldiers only because a woman distracted the soldiers. The soldiers on the truck amused themselves as they were sped along, by trying to hook girls' ankles with a cane."[36]

Lest John Gimbel be accused of exaggerating the problem, *Life* magazine fortuitously provided support for his account when it published a story of its reporters' visit to the University of Marburg. Its article displays a picture of a young woman gamely walking through what looks like a gauntlet of GIs. The caption confirms the impression by stating, "Fraulein strolls by ogling GIs from Marburg redeployment center. GIs have monopolized German girls, robbed and beaten up students and teachers." Given this reality, it is not surprising that the magazine attributes the continued strength of German nationalism among male German students "to the roughneck GIs passing through the local redeployment center."[37]

The 3,500 marriages contracted by late 1948 provide some evidence that a relatively small group of American soldiers and young German women formed romantic attachments—although marriage, too, can be motivated by material circumstances. Nevertheless, Bach's implicit argument that American males and German females were merely exercising their freedom of sexual choice in the chaotic impoverished environment of postwar Germany is extraordinarily self-serving. The combination of desperate poverty and American riches undercut the reality of free choice. Walter Slatoff, writing in *The Nation,* vividly paints the context within which impoverished women linked up with affluent men. "The women of Berlin are hungry, cold, and lonesome. The GI's have cigarettes, which will buy food and coal. The GIs have food—chocolate, doughnuts (taken in large quantities from the Red Cross Clubs). . . . The GIs have warm nightclubs. And the GIs provide a kind of security and meaning in an otherwise meaningless city."[38]

Slatoff's own understanding of the coercion generated by such conditions is not what a feminist analyst would expect:

> The result [of the conditions outlined in the previous quotation] is an aggressive and wholesale manhunt *by the women*. They stand in front of the GI nightclubs, parade up and down the streets in front of the Red Cross clubs and even accost GI's in trolleys, subways, and on the street. "Ich liebe dich" . . . has become no more meaningful than "How do you do?" or "I'm pleased to make your acquaintance." It is very hard for a GI, lonesome and thousands of miles from home, to resist the onslaught, and very easy for him to forget that he is paying for the "love" he receives. When after a few weeks, the sweet "fraulein," like as not the wife of an SS man, weeps that she has no money for coal, or that the "barbaric Russkis" killed her mother and father, took all her possessions, or attacked her, it is almost impossible for her GI sweetheart not to help out or to feel embittered at his former allies. It is important to remember that I am describing not the exception, but the norm in Berlin, and that 90 percent of the soldiers are affected.[39] (My emphasis)

The hostile reaction of some German men to fraternization and the explanation of largely male American commentators for the willing participation of "innocent, helpless" GIs in such activity reveal the existence of two patriarchal stories being constructed in occupied Germany. On the one hand, some of the German population believed that American immorality was turning too-willing German women into whores. On the other hand, many American commentators stressed that naive young American men could not resist the German sophisticated female onslaught. Both narratives portray German women as prostitutes.

Early accounts of fraternization in American journals and newspapers also expressed concern that GI sexual activity would make them prone to Nazi ideology. The innocent surrender of the American male drive to sexually hungry, lascivious young German women inspired ominous as well as humorous reflections. For example, one of *Life*'s first stories on fraternization, the mood switches fast. At first, the text of the story is, at first, meant to be amusing. "There are many complications to what the GIs now call the $65 question. [Sixty-five dollars is the fine for fraternizing.] One complication is that some German girls try to make it as difficult possible for the soldier to behave. There's one blond Fraulein with braided hair who always walked past two MPs every day on her way to do shopping, swinging her hips from side to side even more noticeably than usual. As she passed she would look slyly at the MPs, tap one hip and utter the word 'Verboten.'" But the caption to an accompanying picture on the same page suggests a darker consequence of the easy sexual availability of German women. The picture displays a young woman holding a baby, but the caption undercuts the sentimentality that such an image normally evokes. "This unwed German mother succumbed to the Nazis 'patriotic baby' program. The worried U.S. authorities hope that she and others like her do not switch over to lonely U.S. soldiers."[40]

Many accounts of the German character during this period suggest that the women of the defeated Reich were the carriers of Nazi ideology. Some descriptions of the last resistance to the American onslaught stress the active participation of women.[41] This fear of German women's reactionary nature carried over into the occupation. Tania Long of the *New York Times*, for example, writes that Nazi ideology lay "deeper in their soul" because the strutting of the men during the Nazi period "so impressed Germany's emotionally unstable and highly sentimental women that they completely failed to see where it all was leading the nation."[42]

The portrayal of young German women as solipsistic, dreamy-eyed, *Kinder, Kirche, Kueche* Nazi baby machines lasted for some time, and many Americans worried that soldiers would fall prey to the reactionary sentiments of their "consorts." Surveys do suggest that the soldiers' impressions of Germany became more favorable if they had intense contacts with women. The majority of GIs' behavior indicates, however, that the American soldier did not fall prey to romance and instead constructed a third, more prosaic, straightforward patriarchal understanding of the German woman: She existed to serve the American soldiers' needs.

The recent Nazi past certainly facilitated this interpretive framework. It was easier to think of cigarettes and chocolate as "frau bait"

if the quarry were labeled "fraternazis" or "furleins."[43] Still, the attitude of the soldier stemmed less from the recent German past and
more from the unprecedented ability of young males to pursue sex
in a "favorable" political economic context.

As well, it may be that the Aryan cult of blonde beauties within
American culture had its own stimulating effect on the soldiers.
Harold Zink certainly thought so when he wrote:

> The American GI was of course primarily interested in the German
> Fraulein. After his dreary life in foxholes and his participation in front line
> warfare it is probable that any civilian woman would have seemed attractive.
> The blondness of the German girls in contrast to the tendency of the
> French toward brunette coloring, the adequate wardrobe of the German
> woman in comparison with those of England and France, and the generous
> and warm attitude of many Frauleins did not detract from their desirability
> in the eyes of the American GI. The fact that the silk stockings and finery
> had been looted from women in the rest of Europe or that the willing reac-
> tion on the part of the Fraulein might be an indication of a basic inferior-
> ity in character were rarely taken into account. But the ability of German
> girls to present a fresh and neat appearance in their pastel colored frocks amid
> all of the destruction and chaos and lack of housing was frequently com-
> mented on.[44]

It would be a mistake to think that the gender relationships
described here were only motivated by the unhappy confluence of
young male libido and young, blonde female impoverishment. German women provided more prosaic services as well. A 1946 story in
Life follows a day in the life of Corporal Ralph Gordon of the U.S.
1st Infantry. One of the featured activities is his visit with Annie, the
laundry girl: "Gordon takes his laundry to Annie Haas's home. Only
15, blonde Annie is popular with GIs. Like other Scheinfeld girls she
makes extra money taking in washing."[45] Franklin Davis also notes
that a common joke among troops was that "Fraternization is the
best solution to the laundry problem."[46]

The occupation also relied heavily on household servants who
were paid for by the fledgling German authorities. The jobs were
particularly attractive because servants could get official and unof-

ficial access to American rations. Bach describes three young women from elite backgrounds who worked as servants in the Berlin mansion he visited: "Under the circumstances, they seem tickled pink with their jobs, but if by chance they should not like their present status, they can split the blame between Hitler and their parents."[47]

The Fraternization Problem and the Challenge to the Occupation Army

Even before the conclusion of VE Day, reports indicated that many GIs were turning their attention from fighting to thieving, illegal trading, and sex. Such activity had already strained French–American relations, but at least the new Free French government could take actions to attenuate the tensions and defend its citizens.

The political environment was completely different in occupied Germany for two reasons. First, mass impoverishment combined with the breakdown of ordinary economic intercourse provided far more opportunities for law breaking. Second, the Army itself was the government and had to regulate the behavior of Germans, displaced persons from the workhouses and concentration camps, and soldiers. Troubles in France were serious, but the military authorities could cooperate with the burgeoning French government to control GI behavior. The unruliness of the Americans could be seen as the normal aftermath of war. On the other hand, a failure to establish some modicum of order in Germany called into question the Army's own competence rather than that of a host government.

If the military presence in Germany were to be temporary, this would not be a particularly difficult problem. By early 1946, however, it became increasingly apparent that a sizeable encampment of Army personnel would probably stay in Germany for at least a decade. By 1950, the commitment of soldiers became larger and more open-ended as a result of the heightening tensions associated with the Korean War. This decision to increase the number of soldiers in Germany would not have been possible if the behavior of GIs in the American Zone had not at least become subject to more effective controls. Until 1947, something about the organization and culture of the American postwar Army seemed incompatible with the establishment of law-abiding, self-controlled military units in Germany. The Army had to change the nature of its authority in the occupied land.

Chapter III

The Corrosive Racial Divide

Race Relations in the United States Army
before the Occupation

On August 7, 1918, the headquarters of the Commanding General of the American Expeditionary Force, John "Black Jack" Pershing, issued the following confidential order on the proper handling of black American troops in France:

> We must prevent the rise of any pronounced degree of intimacy between French officers and black officers. We may be courteous and amiable with the last but we cannot deal with them on the same plane as white American officers without deeply wounding the latter. We must not eat with them, must not shake hands with them, seem to talk to them or to meet with them outside the requirements of military service. We must not commend too highly these troops particularly in front of white Americans. Make a point of keeping the native cantonment from spoiling the Negro. White Americans become very incensed at any particular expression of intimacy between white women and black men.[1]

This brief passage reveals much about the nature of white domination within the American Army during the first half of the twentieth century. Army Command was diligent in making certain that black officers and black soldiers recognized their subordinate position within the military. "Amiable courtesy" without shaking hands

or sharing a meal was as hollow a gesture as most of the white officer corps probably meant it to be.

The wording of Pershing Headquarters' directive is bureaucrati-
cally masterful. The authors of the command justify their orders by
emphasizing the deep racial animosity existing within the white
American Army. Those in Pershing's headquarters are not racist—
the authors of the document suggest—but they must worry about
the stability of their authority. It seems that high praise for a black
unit—even if warranted—would have disrupted the discipline of
white soldiers. Even more explosive was the possibility that black
soldiers would have open sexual relations with French women. The
document implies that Pershing and his officers were not motivated
by prejudice, but had to accommodate themselves to the racism of
their white subordinates.

It is probably not a coincidence that this "sociological" perspective also reflected that of General Pershing's Aide-de Camp, future
Chief of Staff, George C. Marshall. Throughout his illustrious
career, Marshall insisted that the military's racial problems originated
within United States society. The Army could not be held responsible for racist practices that it was "compelled" to adopt. The military command's duty was to emphasize efficiency and performance.[2]

Given these views, it is clear that most of those in charge of
Army personnel policies preferred to maintain an all–white army, or
at least an army in which black participation would be strictly limited to a few "traditional" units. By the mid–1930s, this was precisely
the nature of the small, interwar American military. Still, it was
becoming clearer and clearer that the United States might soon be
involved in a new military conflict in Europe and Asia. Once again,
War Department mandarins had to address the question of black
participation in the Army.

The national political context was different in 1940 than it had
been during Woodrow Wilson's segregationist administration. While
Franklin Roosevelt never exhibited the interest in black civil rights
that his wife Eleanor did, he did occasionally respond to pressure
from an increasingly assertive urban black constituency. Thus, Roosevelt announced one month before the 1940 presidential election
that the Army's racial composition would reflect that of the nation.

This meant that the Army anticipated that 10 percent of the military would be African American. Of this group, qualified applicants would be eligible for officer training. Roosevelt also announced that Colonel Benjamin Davis would become the nation's first African American Brigadier General. Finally, FDR appointed the Dean of Howard University's Law School, William Hastie, as a special advisor to the Secretary of War on racial matters.[3]

These announced changes did not really reflect a radical break with the past. Phillip McGuire reports that the 1940 announcement followed an unpublished perspective developed by the War Department's personnel department in 1937, and that the anticipated expansion in black enrollment did not imply a reversal of a system of subordinated segregation.[4] Certainly, Judge Hastie was not impressed with the Army's efforts to integrate blacks into the military. He resigned from his position in early January 1943.[5]

The reality was that even the massive personnel requirements of World War II did not change the Army's policy of keeping whites and blacks apart and of maintaining most black soldiers in menial service occupations. In 1943, 425,000 of 504,000 African American troops were still in the United States. In Europe, very few served in combat. Instead, blacks worked as laborers, truck drivers, and in supply depots. By the end of 1942, only 19.7 percent of black enlisted personnel were in combat units, while 40 percent of white enlisted personnel were in such positions.[6]

Combat experience in Europe was limited to four arenas. Throughout the war, relatively small battalion-sized units were temporarily attached to white combat units for particular engagements. Black field artillery, tank, and tank destroyer units played important support roles for white infantry divisions.[7] In addition to these black battalions, the segregated, black 92nd combat division fought in the bloody Italian campaign, and a segregated unit of black airmen, under the command of General Benjamin Davis' son, participated in air raids in the Southern Mediterranean. Finally, during the desperate days of the Battle of the Bulge, a call went out for the formation of small black platoons to fight alongside exhausted and sometimes overwhelmed white units. It was only this experiment, born out of extraordinary circumstances and limited in time and place, that represented a significant break with the segregationist practice of the Army since the American Civil War.[8]

Despite the small relative numbers, War Department officials evaluated the contribution of African Americans to the war effort almost solely from the perspective of black combat effectiveness. Those supporting the continuation of segregation reasoned that if blacks proved themselves incapable of combat, then their participation in the military should remain in the most subordinated service positions. On the other hand, those military officials concerned with the efficient use of personnel and worried by the extra costs imposed by policies of segregation were interested in examining seriously the fighting effectiveness of the relatively integrated units of the Ardennes.

The limited experience in World War II provided fodder for both segregationists and integrationists. The Italian campaign did not display the 92nd Infantry Division at its best. Some white officers complained that their African American units were reluctant to follow orders which would put them in danger and did not fight effectively when circumstances forced them. (Ironically, it was later discovered that German intelligence had a less racially charged interpretation of the failures of the 92nd. German reports attributed the division's poor performance to inadequate leadership and training.[9]) Similar complaints were made against the black airmen, although here it appears that the Army Air Force ultimately accepted the arguments of Colonel Davis that his unit needed better ground support and more effective training. While there is continuing controversy about the performance of the 92nd Infantry Division, the consensus seems to be that the black airmen acquitted themselves adequately. The ultimate effect of these doubts regarding the quality of the African American combat soldier provided unfortunate support for the many officers who believed in the efficacy of segregation.

There was good reason to challenge the comforting, but racist, conclusion that blacks made poor soldiers. Marcus Ray, who assisted the Assistant Secretary of War, John J. McCloy's, on Army racial issues, concluded that the 92nd Division's poor performance was mainly because of inadequate leadership. Morris MacGregor paraphrases Ray's report: "The basic misconception was that southern white officers understood Negroes; under such officers Negroes who conformed with the southern stereotype were promoted regardless of their abilities, while those who exhibited self-reliance and self-respect—necessary attributes of leadership—were humiliated and discouraged for their uppitiness. 'I was astounded,' he [Ray] said, 'by the willingness of the white officers who preceded us to place their own lives in a hazardous position in order to have tractable Negroes around them.'"[10]

Whatever the precise truth of these claims and counterclaims, the Battle of the Bulge experience provided evidence that seriously undermined segregationist arguments. The emergency call for black troops generated a surprising number of volunteers. Moreover, the African American platoons generally fought well in very dangerous circumstances. MacGregor notes that both the allegedly poor combat performance of the large 92nd Division and the effective performance of the volunteers in the Ardennes could have alerted Army Command to the need to reverse segregationist practices. "In both instances the experiences of World War II had successfully demonstrated to the traditionalists that large-scale segregated units were unacceptable, but neither service was yet ready to accept large-scale integration as an alternative."[11]

The Commanding Officers' Desire to Keep Blacks out of the Early Occupation

Those who would be most responsible for implementing any change in the Army's personnel practices exhibited little interest in integrating the Army during the period of early occupation. After the war's conclusion, Assistant Secretary of War John McCloy distributed a questionnaire which attempted to assess officers' view on the most effective utilization of black troops. The general conclusion was that blacks "performed best as truck drivers, ammunition handlers, stevedores, cooks, bakers, rather than in skilled jobs such as armorer or machinist."[12]

Morris MacGregor perceptively notes that behind these stereotypical views lay the anxious concern of white officers that the

Army would no longer remain a comfortable and secure social institution if the military became integrated. "The stability of the Army
came first; changes would have to be made slowly, without risking
the menace of disruption. An attempt to mix the races in the Army
seemed to most officers a dangerous move bordering on irresponsi-
bility. Furthermore, the majority of Army officers, dedicated to the
traditions of the service, saw the Army as a social as well as military
institution. It was a way of life that embraced families, wives, and
children. . . . Why then should the old patterns be modified; why
exchange comfort for possible chaos?"[13]

At the conclusion of World War II, the preference of most Army
officers was to implement a policy which would once again weed
out black soldiers from their command despite the fact that the
Army had just recently published literature and sponsored a movie
directed by Frank Capra that challenged racist stereotyping.[14] Certainly, the most important generals in charge of the occupation of
Germany exhibited no interest in promoting the significant participation of blacks outside of traditionally segregated fields. A delegation of the Negro Newspaper Publishers Association reported in
May 1946 that: "[Blacks] were conspicuously absent from the ETO
headquarters, Frankfurt. If they were stationed near, they had no
official duties in Frankfurt. Not a single Negro officer appeared to
be on the staff of General Joseph T. McNarney. In like manner, we
found no Negroes in military government."[15]

One gets the impression that General McNarney wished not to
be bothered with racial issues. When confronted with blatant discrimination that violated Army relations, the General would
respond. However, he would take no positive action to eliminate
racial subordination. Thus, Army Command tolerated the refusal of
a Red Cross Club located near USFET headquarters to serve blacks
until this illegal form of segregation was brought to the attention of
Army commanders by the Negro Newspaper Publishers Association. McNarney stopped this rather common Red Cross practice,
but the fact that such an important institution for the morale of soldiers was allowed to exclude Americans from service does not speak
well for the diligence of those in charge of USFET headquarters.[16]
(It should be noted that the Red Cross's treatment of blacks during

World War II was shameful. The organization even went to the extent of segregating blood donations.[17])

In addition to General McNarney's, the commander of the European Theater, apparent disinterest in racial issues, General Lucius Clay also did not worry himself about the lack of African Americans in his occupation government. The man in charge of occupation government believed that black units should be employed solely as parade troops. Similarly, General Ernest Harmon, the commander of the Constabulary, strongly supported the War Department decision that only white soldiers need apply to this elite police unit. Finally, as we shall see, General Geoffrey Keyes, commander of the Third Army, the major occupation force in Germany, assiduously worked to reduce the number of African Americans under his command.

The general desire on the part of the key commanding officers, as well as most of their immediate subordinates, to keep African American soldiers at some distance from the units with which they worked most closely suggests that the attitudes of those in charge of the occupation army in 1946 were not very far removed from the sordid perspectives of General John Pershing's Headquarters in 1918. Blacks might have to be tolerated, but their presence was undesirable. What the Army officers did not realize was that the attempt to reinforce segregation was incompatible with the new security requirements of the German occupation.

Forces for Change

Desirable or not, Army Command had to confront circumstances far different from those that had existed after World War I. In fact, important commanders of the Army would eventually come to realize that the successful maintenance of the Army in Germany would require a significant revision of the racist policies with which most officers were comfortable.

Three factors were especially important in challenging Army policy. First, patterns of demobilization and reenlistment meant that the European Theater was likely to absorb an increasing percentage of African American troops. Second, the Military faced more consistent pressure from black public opinion to change its personnel policies. And third, the racial oppression associated with the segregated Army was imposing unacceptable costs on the occupation mission.

The initial personnel crisis stemmed from the demobilization plan that gave preference to those soldiers who had been in combat. Very few African American troops could qualify for immediate shipment back home, and this tended to raise the percentage of black soldiers in the occupation army. Furthermore, the postwar period saw blacks reenlisting and enlisting at a disproportionately high rate. Despite the clear discrimination African Americans faced in the Army, the evidence suggests that a segment of the young adult, black male population was drawn to the Army because many felt safer in the military and were worried about returning to an unstable economy and possibly violent society. The experience of the Depression still weighed heavily on many soldiers'—black and white—minds, but African Americans also remembered the wave of lynching, which swept through the South between World War I and World War II.

Because of those factors, "the percentage of Negroes in the Army rose above its wartime high of 9.68% of the enlisted strength and was expected to reach 15% and more by 1947."[18] Many in the Army were dismayed by these trends. To put the matter bluntly, leading officers believed that they would soon have too few white soldiers and too many black soldiers. The major European and East Asian commands were under particular pressure to absorb a disproportionate number of African American GIs because informal and formal agreements prevented the Army from sending black troops to the Panama Canal Zone, Iceland, the Azores and China.[19] For this reason, the War Department decided that the European and Asian Theaters would have to have an Army whose personnel was at least 15 percent black.

The anticipated relative expansion of African American troops in the Army pressured War Department officials to consider some revision in their policies of segregation. On September 27, 1945, the new Secretary of War, Robert P. Patterson, called for an officer board to review the manpower use of African Americans. George

Marshall appointed Lieutenant General Alvan C. Gillem, Jr., to head the task force. The committee concluded its deliberations by calling for the proportionate utilization of black soldiers in all military occupations and the creation of integrated units at the Division level. Below this, it was believed that blacks and whites should continue to be placed in smaller segregated units. The Army released the Gillem report to the press on March 4, 1946, and published the task force's recommendations as policy approximately eight weeks later, on April 27. By this time, Marshall had left Army service and the new Chief of Staff, Dwight Eisenhower, was, at best, only slightly more sympathetic to the demands of racial justice.

These cautious internal calls for some modest reform in the Army practice of segregation also responded to increasing pressure from black political leaders and opinion-makers who argued for the immediate integration of the Armed Forces. The appointment of Judge William Hastie as a special assistant to the War Department on racial matters had not led to any rapid reversal in Army practices. Nevertheless, Hastie's angry resignation from his position had not diminished black influence. More tractable African American advocates, Truman Gibson and then Marcus Ray, replaced the Dean of the Howard University Law school within the War Department and continued to press more circumspectly for changes in Army policy. Moreover, the African American press consistently published its dissatisfaction with Army racial policies. Especially enraging were reports "that circulated in the black press in 1945 [which] described German prisoners of war being fed in a railroad restaurant while their black Army guards were forced to eat outside."[20]

At the conclusion of World War II, this press demonstrated continued interest in the status of African American soldiers in Europe and Japan. During May 1946, Frank L. Stanley, president, Dowdal H. Davis, Jr., vice-president, and William O. Walker, past president of the Negro Newspaper Publishers Association toured Europe and sent their report to the relatively sympathetic Secretary of War Patterson. Their denunciation of racist practices within the Army led to an impassioned advocacy for the rapid integration of units and commands (especially of Military Police), the immediate elimination of inequitable facilities, the orientation of all troops on race issues, the expansion of educational opportunities, the stationing and utilization of blacks in key cities, aggressive campaigns against venereal disease and the excessive usage of alcohol, and the removal of prisoners of war from positions of trust.[21]

This report conflicted with two other significant studies of the early occupation. On the one hand, noted criminologist Leonard Keeler concluded his study for the Army's Criminal Investigation Division by arguing that blacks should be completely removed from Europe. This view was not an aberration. An investigation conducted on behalf of the Senate's War Investigation Committee (known as the Meader report) also concluded in late 1946 that, "The War Department [should] give careful consideration to the recommendation of its field commanders. The European commander was already on record with a recommendation to recall all black troops from Europe, citing the absence of Negroes from the U.S. Occupation Army in the Rhineland after World War I."[22] Many white Americans from within and outside the Army continued to believe that there should be no black military presence in Europe.[23]

Racial Conflict in the Early Days of the Occupation

The precipitous decline in discipline associated with the conclusion of World War II could not but deleteriously affect race relations within the Army. As African American Chester Jones, Staff Sergeant of the 3418th Trucking Company (popularly called the Red Ball Express) within George Patton's Third Army stated, after VE Day, "The old racial bug-a-boo came back in full force."[24] The increase of racial conflicts was owed to three factors. First, organizational confusion in the postwar Army made it very difficult for officers to know what their troops were actually doing during the day. Second, the lack of specific duties for many awaiting demobilization led to the excessive use of liquor and an intensified competition for sexual access to women. Finally, the intense desire to get home on initially scarce shipping space worsened racial relations as idle units waited to leave Europe.

Sergeant Jones's, perhaps, apocryphal memory of a spectacular racial incident in Bremen synthesizes all the points I have made so far:

> When the war ended we were sent to Bremerhaven in preparation for our eventual return to the United States. . . . At night we would go to Bremen . . . for entertainment. I ran into a lot of my trucking buddies there. One night they rented a cafe for a party and several of us at Bremerhaven were invited. Two of the truckers went to pick up their girls. They stopped at a bar en route to have a drink. At the bar they encountered a group of whites from the 29th Division. Any Negro in Europe during World War II knows the 29th. It was an all-cracker division that had a real "thing" about blacks. In Bremen Negro soldiers did not go out on the streets alone at night because they not only got stomped but members of the 29th enjoyed killing them.
>
> My two friends who had stopped in the bar were forced to do a jig while these crackers shot at their feet, the ceiling, everywhere. The truckers were finally sent on their way with shots to encourage their haste. They returned to the party and told what had happened. About twenty-five men at the party returned to the scene of the jig and shot it up. Five or six of the 29th bit the dust. The fellows from the party quickly returned to the party and gave their guns to the German cafe owner, who hid them. In about six minutes the places was swarming with MPs and their officers. They took all of us to a school building and lined us up. They picked up all the Negroes they ran into within a half-dozen square blocks of our cafe. Two MPs came in with two Negro soldiers saying they just entered the area. The captain in charge said, "Bring them in anyway and line them up with the rest of the niggers." After making us stand a while they brought in the men of the 29th who had been at OK Corral and had not been shot. They were to identify the assailants, but as you know . . . , we all look alike so they were unable to single out one man. I have an idea making Negro soldiers do the jig did not long remain a favorite form of entertainment among the men of the 29th.[25]

Given these events, it is not surprising that Sergeant Jones was "the happiest man on earth when he received his discharge papers."[26]

Relations with the German Population

Experiences were not all negative for black soldiers in Europe. Despite white American hostility, the reception of the European civilian population was often friendly. Indeed, the reports of both Marcus Ray and the Negro Newspaper Publishers Association delegation stressed that the reaction of the German population to the African American presence was surprisingly hospitable.

The expectation was that blacks would experience widespread hostility as a result of the virulent racism of Nazi ideology. Indeed, white officers often used the Nazi experience as an excuse to limit the black presence in Germany and to exclude those who were there from participating in the military police and the constabulary. Ray's comment on this argument clearly lays the blame for racial difficulties where it belonged:

> Because of racial ideologies of the German people, it was thought inexpedient to assign Negro personnel to the constabulary as this assignment would require supervision and police control over German nationals.
>
> To accept the racial prejudices of the German people as a reason for the nonutilization of the American soldier who happens to be nonwhite is to negate the very ideals we have made a part of our reeducation program in Germany. In talking with representative German nationals, such as the burgomeisters and police representatives, I found no carry-over of Nazi racial ideologies directed against the American Negro soldier. The expected ideological difficulties in the use of Negro troops in Germany have not materialized. In those areas, for example, Graffenwoehr, where only Negro soldiers are located, the German youth program is progressing as well under the direction of colored soldiers as in other parts of Germany where only white troops are stationed.[27]

Advocates for civil rights had learned that the real source of racism came from the "democratic" American forces. Surprisingly, the German population in general did not seem to make the same extreme invidious distinctions between black and white Americans. In this, they seemed to behave more like the British population when huge numbers of Americans "occupied" that island before D-Day.[28]

This is not to say that black soldiers experienced no conflict with the native populations, but it would be incorrect to see such clashes as an inevitable product of indigenous racism about which the Army could do nothing. Army policies inevitably exacerbated the tensions which did exist from racial stereotyping. For example:

In April 1946 . . . soldiers of the 449th Signal Construction Detachment threw stones at two French officers who were driving through the village of Weyersbusch, in the Rhine Palatinate. The officers, one of them injured, returned to the village with French MP's and requested an explanation of the incident. They were quickly surrounded by about thirty armed Negroes of the detachment who, according to the French, acted in an aggressive and menacing manner. As a result, the Supreme French Commander in Germany requested his American counterpart to remove all black troops from the French zone. The U.S. commander in Europe, General Joseph T. McNarney, investigated the incident, court-martialed its instigators, and transferred the entire detachment out of the French zone. At the same time his staff explained to the French that to prohibit the stationing of Negroes in the area would be discriminatory and contrary to Army policy. Black specialists continued to operate in the French zone, although none were subsequently stationed there permanently.[29]

Despite the Army's careful statement that black soldiers would not suffer from the arbitrary exclusion from the French zone of the Rhineland Palatinate, it is clear that the commanding officers in Frankfurt bowed to French pressures (perhaps with eagerness) and thus reinforced the view that black soldiers as such were the reason for any significant problems of indiscipline.

Racially charged conflicts with other occupying forces were not too common since the different national armies in Germany tried to ensure that their soldiers stayed within their own zones. In any event, there is no evidence that many members of the other occupying forces had strongly developed racist sentiments against black Americans. Far more common were complex clashes involving black soldiers, German women, German men, and white American GIs.

A reading of the documents suggests that during the early occupation, periodic racial disturbances took one of two forms. The first type involved small-scale fights or brawls. These would regularly occur in bars on weekends, when a German male might object to the "monopolization" of young German women by American soldiers. This issue only had a potential racial dimension when black soldiers (and perhaps other Americans of non European origin) were involved in such conflicts. The record suggests that these brawls were frequent and that blacks were involved in them. On the other hand, the early occupation records also reveal that the German population which was involved in these disputes was more likely to interpret such clashes as an American–German problem rather than a black–white issue. As Morris MacGregor states: "It was only later that the Germans, especially tavern owners and the like, began to adopt the discriminatory practices of their conquerors."[30]

The racializing of these endemic sexual conflicts more often than not came from the Americans. Thus, the Negro Newspaper Publishers Association reports: "On the question of MPs, we received numerous complaints about their persistent efforts to discourage association with the white population, particularly women. Strong-arm methods are employed at the mere sight of a Negro soldier and a white girl, regardless of her character. . . . . Actual testimony freely given to us by many civilians reveals their unwillingness to discriminate."[31]

The second type of conflict which involved the German population was more overtly racial. Here, specific groups of German women and American blacks found themselves pitted against German men and women who did find the large number of relationships between German women and black American men to be offensive. Rather than brawls between sexually active males, these clashes more often took the form of public street confrontations.

During March and April 1946, the Nurnberg area seemed to be plagued with such incidents. The Public Safety Officer in Regierungsbezirk Ober-und Mittelfranken reported: "At Weissenburg colored soldiers assaulted a woman and her minor sons for insulting their girl friends in public."[32] One week later, the same military government official reported that there were "19 cases of assault upon German civilians by military personnel; most cases were perpetrated by colored American troops."[33] It is likely that the high incidence of violent crimes committed by African Americans were fueled by these endemic conflicts, which were in turn exacerbated by the hostile reactions of white military police.

Finally, there were some racial incidents which were more explicitly political, but once again centered around the sexual activity of African American soldiers. Such conflicts typically began with the jailing of German women who normally had sexual relations with black American men. Evidence is scattered, but anecdotal reports suggest that such "camp followers" with connections to black soldiers were more likely to live as squatters in sordid camps outside the environs of German villages and cities. The presence of these impoverished women raised a variety of concerns for American military government officers and an American-approved group of local politicians. Campaigns to control VD and preserve "public morality" intersected and led to occasional attempts to clear out the female shanty towns located near military encampments. Such actions led to the incarceration or removal of the women living in these hovels. Less dramatic incidents included the jailing of groups of women who could not present a legitimate reason for being in the area.[34]

The records tell us that African American soldiers often reacted angrily to these round-ups. Sometimes, there were attempts by small numbers of soldiers to free the imprisoned women. At Ansbach, for example: "Two colored American soldiers broke into the local jail, assaulted the jailer, and tried to release a woman prisoner."[35]

Other times, the conflicts were more dramatic. Several reports in the official records describe groups of angry African American GIs demonstrating in front of jails or city halls demanding the release of those women who had been incarcerated. In a personal communication to me, for example, Dr. Arthur Volz—who in the previous chapter described his VD control strategy while serving as a Captain in Weilburg, Hesse—reports that he had to confront a demonstration of black soldiers who were demanding the release of women from the local jail. Volz reports that it was with some trepidation that he intervened, since he and fellow white occupation officers were the only white Americans on the scene. The white officers of the black unit only arrived later, and Volz notes that they were not up to the job.[36]

Crime and Venereal Disease

The previous chapter revealed that the struggle to control VD was a response to a very real problem. Moreover, this crisis disproportionately affected the black soldier. The majority of white officers came into positions of command already assuming that African Americans made inferior soldiers. The significantly greater suffering of black soldiers from venereal disease combined with the higher rate of criminal behavior could not but reinforce these prejudices and thus exacerbate racial relations. As Morris MacGregor notes:

> By any measures of discipline and morale, black soldiers as a group posed a serious problem to the Army in the postwar period. The standard military indexes—serious incidents statistics, venereal disease rates, and number of courts-martial—revealed black soldiers in trouble out of all proportion to their percentage of the Army's population. When these personal infractions and crimes were added to the riots and serious racial incidents that continued to occur in the Army all over the world after the war, the dimensions of the problem became clear.[37]

VD rates were high for both whites and blacks. In general, the rates were three times greater than those reported for soldiers in the United States.[38] Blacks came into the Army with greater infection rates, and military historian Ulysses Grant Lee maintains that the VD rate of black American troops was often lower than that of the black civilian population in the South. (He attributes the high rate to the failure of the U.S. Public Health Service to treat the Southern black population during the late 1930s.)[39] Given this historical condition, it is not surprising that African American venereal disease rates were higher than those for white soldiers. Still, the difference is very large. Table 3.1 suggests that even when black rates began to decline during the fall of 1946, they remained about three times as large as those for whites.

It is important to note that there is no compelling evidence that black's sexual activity was significantly different than whites'. Thus, the reason for the higher rate must be inadequate treatment. This is true in three ways. First, African American soldiers found it more difficult to obtain replacements for the venereal disease prophylactic and treatment kits (V-Kits) that were an essential item for the occupation soldier. Second, the inadequate leadership of black units probably translated into much poorer efforts to educate the soldiers about the causes of venereal disease. Finally, the women who had relations with black soldiers also suffered from inadequate treatment. The evidence is that the German women who consorted with blacks were less likely to be treated generously by German or American authorities. Relations were thus more illicit and more difficult to regulate.[40]

Complaints about the criminal behavior of African American troops also gave rise to the usual assortment of charges that African American troops were unsuitable for military duty. Certainly, the crime rate data collected by European Command portrays a daunting reality. The following table (3.1) reveals that even though blacks were only 9.35 percent of the total European Army in 1946, the proportion of African American GIs charged with offenses was consistently higher than their share in the military population.

Within the military offense category, only the combat-related offense "misbehavior before the enemy" yielded a relatively low percentage. This is due to the fact that relatively few African Americans had been involved in combat during the war. On the other hand, the fact that 49.6 percent of those charged with "discreditable conduct before a superior" were black suggests that officers were much more sensitive to signs of insubordination within the African American units.

Within the civil affairs crime categories, the high murder (62.2 percent of those charged), assault (59.0 percent) and rape (53.1 percent) figures are less easy to explain. These were crimes which were by and large committed against the German population, not against those white soldiers most responsible for racial subordination. Mac-Gregor states: "The most common explanation offered for such statistics is that fundamental injustices drove the black servicemen to crime. Probably more to the point, most black soldiers, especially during the early postwar period, served in units burdened with many disadvantaged individuals, soldiers more likely to get into

Table 3.1 The Proportion of African American GI Crimes in Europe 1946

(% of crimes committed by African Americans)

Military Offenses	
AWOL	13.4
Desertion	17.4
Misbehavior before enemy	1.9
Violation of arrest or confinement	12.6
Discreditable conduct toward superior	49.6
Civil Offenses	
Murder	62.2
Rape	53.1
Robbery	33.1
Manslaughter	46.3
Burglary and Housebreaking	29.0
Larceny	17.2
Forgery	8.9
Assault	59.0

Source: Morris J. MacGregor, *Integration of the Armed Forces, 1940–1965.* (Washington, D.C.: Center of Military History, 1981): 207.

trouble given the characteristically weak leadership in these units. But another explanation for at least some of these crime statistics hinged on commanders' power to define serious offenses."[41]

It is certainly plausible that white officers were more likely to believe a German woman's claim of rape if the alleged perpetrator was black.[42] This probably does not mean that African American soldiers did not commit some of the rapes with which they were charged. Rather, officers were more likely to interpret black contacts with the female population hostilely, while forgiving white soldiers for their "youthful indiscretions." For many officers, sexual relations between black soldiers and German women constituted an egregious harm to the social order even if the black and white participants consented to the relationship. White soldiers were more likely to avoid rape charges even when they were guilty of the crime.

The gap in the murder and assault rates, however, also implies that African American soldiers were more likely to be involved in other violent crimes. As before, it is possible that African American soldiers were held to a higher standard than white GIs. The crime rate of white soldiers could be understated, since the classification of violent incidents depended on officer discretion.

Despite these statistical difficulties, it is likely that blacks were more likely to engage in violent criminal acts for two reasons. First, the superior mobility of black transportation units gave the individual soldier more opportunity to commit crimes of property as well as related crimes of violence. As late as January and February 1947, when the Third Army was being "closed out," the "Report of Operations" noted:

> There are increasing indications that United States soldiers, especially Negro troops, are actively participating in black market enterprises. Arrests during the period clearly depict a chain of supply of American scrip to a Displaced Persons gang, who in turn make resale of scrip either to Displaced Persons or German civilians at scandalous prices (13,000 Reich marks for a hundred dollars). Evidence of sale of United States property on the black market such as tires (selling at 1,000 marks each) was also uncovered during the period. There are sections of the Displaced Persons and Civilian population continuing to sell schnapps to United States soldiers for cigarettes, candy, or scrip, which are then bartered on the black market for any other items which the individuals may deem essential.[43]

Ironically, blacks were in a better position to supply these goods from American supplies because of their restriction to warehouses and transportation pools. Because of the large profits that could be made, it is not surprising that soldiers who took advantage of the opportunity were also more likely to use violence to protect their economic autonomy. Certainly, Army officers worried continuously about their ability to supervise transportation units. One section from the Third Army's "Report of Operations" during the second quarter of 1946 is particularly revealing:

> An analysis of the causes of the more serious administrative problems during the quarter shows that a lack of officers and an over strength of untrained enlisted men is the basis of most difficulties. It is a physical impossibility for

one or two officers to run a truck company properly, train drivers, run motor stables, and carry on training programs as prescribed. With regard to enlisted men, the two Transportation Corps Trucking Groups in Third Army Zone in May, for example, had a total strength (enlisted) of 7,420. Ninety percent are colored, which in itself is a problem. To complicate the situation still more, these groups were ordered, in the latter part of May, to absorb a 20% over strength of colored personnel. Most of these men are fresh from the States, had a minimum of training and will require very close supervision to make soldiers out of them. A high rate of incidents in Transportation Corps units can be expected until these corrections are made.[44]

The greater opportunity to commit crimes is only one part of a full explanation of the greater incidence of criminal activity among African Americans. A second reason must focus on the more profound alienation of black troops from military authority. The rules of the Army carried less legitimacy within the black rank and file. The 1943 Army poll referred to earlier found that a lower percentage of black soldiers believed in the war effort and a higher percentage were much more aware of the inequities of racial discrimination in the Army.[45] Oral histories of black soldiers' experience during World War II also suggest that the typical African American GI was more skeptical of white officers' intentions and more likely to take actions which would violate the racist social order so basic to the Army during this period. It is significant that efforts by commanding officers to treat blacks more favorably resulted in a significant reduction in the crime rate of black soldiers. (See Chapter VI.) Whatever the reasons, during the first two years: "Black soldiers consistently dominated the Army's serious incident rate, a measure of indictments and accusations involving troops in crimes against persons and property. In June 1946, for example, black soldiers in the European theater were involved in serious incidents (actual and alleged) at the rate of 2.57 cases per 1,000 men. The rate among white soldiers for the same period was .79 cases per 1,000 men. The rate for both groups rose considerably in 1947. The figure of Negroes climbed to a yearly average of 3.94 incidents per 1,000; the figure for whites, reflecting an even greater gain reached 1.88."[46]

Given the reality of the higher relative number of crimes committed by black soldiers and given the hostility of many white officers to the black presence in Germany, it is not surprising that the incarceration rate of African American soldiers was very high. During 1945, blacks were 17 percent of the total prison population, and in 1946, more than a quarter of the incarcerated population was black.[47] In addition, during the third quarter of 1946, black soldiers were three times more likely to be court martialed than whites. This occurred even though the relative presence of black Americans in the occupation Army began to decline after June 1946 and even though records indicate that white criminality increased at a faster rate during 1946.[48]

Even more disturbing than these incarceration figures is the report from the Negro Publishers Association, which indicates that black soldiers suffered even more disproportionately from capital punishment. "In May 1946, Louis Lautier, chief of Negro Newspaper Publishers Association news service, informed the Assistant Secretary of War that fifty-five of the seventy American soldiers executed for crimes in the European Theater were black. Most were category IV and V men."[49]

The Drive to Remove Blacks from Germany

In 1946, most of those in charge of the Army did not view these figures as a product of racial discrimination. Rather, they felt that the problem lay in the nature of the black troops themselves. Even advocates of African American interests such as Marcus Ray conceded that many poor blacks were unsuitable for military service because their performance on aptitude or intelligence tests placed them in the bottom fortieth percentile. (These were the category IV and V men.) Ray endorsed efforts to drive such men out of the Armed Forces, while encouraging skilled blacks to compete for all jobs in the Army.

Many white officers and commentators did not make such careful distinctions between suitable and unsuitable "colored" troops. For example, when the War Department announced in early 1946 that 15 percent of the personnel in the major European and Asian commands would be African American: "Both commands (European and Asian) protested the War Department decision. Representatives from the European Theater arrived in Washington in mid-February 1946 to propose a black strength of 8.21 rather than the prescribed 15 percent. Seeking to determine where black soldiers could be used "with the least harmful effect on theater operations," they discovered in conferences with representatives of the War Department staff only the places Negroes were not to be used: in infantry units, in the constabulary, which acted as a border patrol and occupation police, in highly technical services, or as supervisors of white civilian laborers."[50]

The irrationality of this decision is a testament to the strength of racial prejudice within the Army. At the same time that Army commanders chronically complained about the shortage of skilled personnel to execute needed occupation tasks, the same officers consistently refused to consider making training available to black soldiers so that they could perform these tasks. The decision to prevent African Americans from guarding white laborers is particularly revealing. Army Command seemed to be saying that blacks had less social prestige and perhaps authority than those unfortunates in displaced persons camps or who were prisoners of war.

Despite the almost nonsensical implications of limiting blacks to particular subordinate assignments, the commanding officers of the Third Army were clearly pleased by the War Department's decision to exclude blacks from traditional white jobs, even though this violated the War Department's own personnel policy as outlined in the Gillem report. During the first half of 1946, the Third Army leadership vigorously implemented policies to exclude blacks from supervisory and even some relatively menial occupations. During the second quarter of 1946, for example, the Third Army Chief of Staff advised the 514th Quartermaster Group: "That it was the recommendation of this Headquarters that colored personnel not be used in administrative positions at Group level, as experience has shown that white troops are more satisfactory in these positions."[51]

Even more startling was the Third Army's decision to exclude black troops from postal service duties. At a time when the number of black troops was rising (April–June 1946): "The Chief of Staff announced a policy of using only white personnel as drivers in transporting and handling mail. In concurrence with this policy, a provisional truck company was formed to provide transportation and drivers for all mail runs which must be made by truck. This provisional truck company will be attached to Headquarters Special Troops. This action will materially decrease transportation time and will insure reliability and proper handling and safeguarding of mail."[52]

Given these actions, it is not surprising that the Third Army's commanding general, Geoffrey Keyes, lobbied vigorously for a rapid reduction in the number of black troops under his command. By July, he was finally successful. "At the request of this Headquarters, Headquarters USFET requested the War Department to refrain from sending colored troops in excess of the OTB for training to this zone. As a result, all surplus colored personnel are to be shipped to the ZI during the latter part of August."[53] (*ZI* stands for Zone of the Interior. This means the continental United States.) Keyes was pleased with this decision since he firmly believed that: "[The] Integration of colored troops should not be carried out as an experiment in the occupational zone of Germany."[54]

Such decisions for Germany led to changes in policy in Washington as well. During this period, the Army tried to persuade the Selective Service not to call blacks for the draft. A more substantive decision was made by Assistant Secretary of War (and future Secretary of State) Dean Rusk, who in concert with the Secretary of War "suspended enlistment of blacks in regular Army—except for those qualified for specialties in which there was personnel shortage."[55]

By October, the concerted effort to restrict the black presence in Germany became even more severe. The Adjutant General announced that African American enlistees would have to score *higher* on the Army's aptitude test in order to be accepted in the Army. Moreover, the black men who passed this hurdle would no longer have the right to choose where they would serve as soldiers.

The most charitable interpretation one can make of General Keyes' and the Pentagon's actions is that the military leadership hoped the reduction in the number of black soldiers would attenuate many of the difficulties caused by the GI presence in Germany.

It apparently escaped the notice of all the commanding generals and their civilian backers that this policy of elimination and subordination actually exacerbated conditions within the Army. Very soon after the successful execution of General Keyes' policy, the Army would reverse itself and implement one of the first Affirmative Action programs in American history.

Chapter IV

From Colony to Junior Partner

Modern German and Cold War historians have long discussed the rapid evolution of American postwar policy toward Germany. The August 1945 Potsdam accord anticipated that Germany would make extensive reparation payments, receive no reconstruction aid, and be subject to extensive economic and political controls. Secretary of State George Marshall's proposal of an extensive foreign aid program for Europe changed this punitive vision. In fact, it is generally agreed that the basic framework for the Marshall Plan was in place by late 1946. In September of that year, then Secretary of State James Byrnes had articulated in Stuttgart a much more conciliatory vision of Germany's future in the world community. By early 1947, the British and Americans had created a unified West German territory called the Bizonia, which now concentrated on economic rejuvenation.

Much of this startling transformation is no doubt explained by geopolitical calculation. Germany throughout the Cold War remained the key European flashpoint. It did not take long for both emerging superpowers to realize that it was in each of their interests to construct a German nation friendly to them. If it were impossible to dominate the complete postwar German territory, then a large section of it would have to do. The breakup of Germany required both the United States and the Soviet Union to find and mold Germans who could attain some internal political legitimacy and represent the interests of the superpower. At the same time, the rival occupation Armies would have to play a much less visible role in the regulation of German political life.

This institutional transformation of the military was not automatic. Indeed, it was the good fortune of American policymakers that the incompetence of the early postwar occupation forces did not seriously disrupt American efforts to establish a stable military presence in Germany. A major reason for this eventual success was that circumstances forced Army officials to implement helter-skelter policies that laid the basis for West Germany's future alliance with the United States. Financial pressures, personnel crises, and economic disarray forced military officials to turn over some of the reins of power to eager German actors waiting in the wings—even though this devolution of authority often took place without the knowledge or approval of high officials in Washington. Chaotic social conditions were the irrational stimuli of the evolution of a more effective American foreign policy in Germany.

The Turn to German Collaborators

Edward Peterson has written that, after extensive archival work in the German provinces, he came to this "humbling conclusion": "The occupation's 'action' occurred largely in Clay's headquarters and consisted primarily of Americans arguing with Americans about what could or should be done. . . . The American victory in the occupation seems in essence a retreat from policies based on interference that would not work to other policies based on noninterference."[1]

We should not understand this process as a straightforward result of rational calculation. A primary reason for American withdrawal resulted from the inability to execute more aggressive tasks. Within Germany, the confusion associated with the redeployment and demobilization of American troops eroded almost all organizational stability. The officer corps of the occupation government, despite rather elaborate training experiences in the United States and England, were also eligible for redeployment. Harold Zink writes, for example, that officers trained in military government obtained releases from service even though they were considered critical to the military's new mission. Zink notes that the results could have been disastrous. "At a very critical period American military government in Germany found itself without adequate personnel, forced to rely on any officer available for assignment whether trained in anything relating to military government or not."[2]

Redeployment policy resulted in enormous turnover within military government. By the end of 1945, 40 percent of the occupation government officers and 50 percent of the enlisted men were eligible for demobilization.[3] In the university town of Marburg, for example, there were 12 military governors between 1945 and 1952. Some of them were barely remembered by the townspeople, and few made any imprint. This experience is not anomalous. Peterson reports similarly rapid turnover in his studies of the provinces during the occupation period.[4]

It was also not easy to get transfers of qualified officers. Zink argues that tactical units before VJ Day were only willing to give up "psycho-neurotics" to military government. After VJ Day, colonels eager to maintain their position in the postwar Army looked for a sinecure in Germany, whether or not they had any training in occupation government. Zink writes that: "Their main concern was that they receive the most palatial quarters that they live in a style fitting their positions."[5]

Perhaps only a small minority of those in the occupation government were "rascals and looters," but the lack of a clear policy, the lack of clear support from the rest of the Army in Germany, poor equipment, and discrimination against the older officers trained in military government led to a less than impressive governing regime.[6] Given this confusion, it is not hard to see how American soldiers within the occupation government lost initiative, even though creative actions in the field were probably more important in this military endeavor than in combat.[7]

The decline in trained American personnel did not mean that the responsibilities facing the occupation government had diminished. During the summer of 1945, the early occupation authorities faced mountainous tasks. Unlike Japan, there was no governing structure at all after the collapse of Hitler's government. Entering military government detachments had to restore local administration by appointing a Burgermeister (or the equivalent local political leader) who could then, with some Army assistance, reconstruct the economic infrastructure. In addition, the first military governors had to requisition housing for Army personnel as well as enforce the bans on fraternization between Americans and Germans and black marketing activity.

Most of these officers had no ability to speak or understand German. The result was a heavy reliance on German "collaborators" right at the beginning of the occupation. John Gimbel writes that the quality of these initial assistants often frustrated American efforts to construct a conservative, capitalist society. "[The occupation authorities] were immediately faced with the complete collapse of civil authority. . . . They were hampered by their own personnel policies and by the fact they had to rely upon German employees with little training, little experience, little stake in the community, and with strong leftist political leanings.[8]

In addition, each occupation unit had to respond to enormous bureaucratic demands from higher occupation authorities. Earl Ziemke reports, for example, that the average detachment dispatched 305 reports of one kind or another during one month in late 1945.[9] Such paperwork further isolated the American contingents from the German population.

The Army "responded" to these personnel problems in three ways. First, the number of Americans working in military government declined sharply. Second, within this shrinking American workforce, civilians took on a larger and larger percentage of the governing authorities. Indeed, Lucius Clay at first wanted to "civilianize" the military government personnel completely by the end of 1945.[10] Finally, German employees increasingly took on the crucial tasks of the occupation government for the Americans.

Table 4.1 outlines the rapid decline both in American personnel and in the relative number of officers and enlisted soldiers working in the occupation government. The increased emphasis on employing Germans was even more dramatic. Oliver Frederiksen describes the evolution well: "During the summer of 1945 the official ban

Table 4.1   The Decline in American Staffed Military Government

	9/30/45	9/30/46	9/30/47	9/30/4	9/30/49
Number of U.S. Personnel in Military Government	11,943	5,459	3,874	2,629	2,104
% Military	98.5	53.3	36.5	8.1	1.2

Source: Oliver J. Frederiksen, *The American Military Occupation of Germany, 1945–53* (Headquarters, United States Army, Europe, Historical Division, 1953): 33.

against employing Germans was lifted. German civilians now provided an unlimited source of cheap and competent labor. By September 1945 their employment priority had been moved up to follow that of American civilians already in the theater. In November permission was given to use them in positions [which] have access to information classified as high as 'confidential,' and in exceptional cases even higher. German guards used to protect military supplies and installations could be armed."[11]

The Army's occupation pamphlet for incoming soldiers, which was cited earlier, reminded the GIs that there were also some good Germans. The armed civil police, in particular, needed to be treated with respect. "Don't be surprised when you see them carrying arms; they need them. . . . By recognizing them as agents of Military Government and showing respect for the job they are doing, you make your own work easier."[12]

The Success Behind Denazification's Failure

The personnel crisis had its most immediate impact on the policies that were meant to restructure German politics. The denazification drive slowed and sputtered to a confusing halt within a year and a half, while the efforts to construct representative governmental institutions moved much faster than anticipated.

Contrary to some mythology, a case could be made that the American authorities were initially more determined than their

Allied counterparts to punish Nazi officials and exclude them from positions of influence in the new society.[13] The Army's ban on fraternization with Germans was mainly motivated by a conviction that Germans were collectively responsible for Nazi outrages against humanity. The determination to punish German society intensified after the discovery of the concentration camps. "Whatever doubts OMGUS [Office of Military Government–United States] may have had about the necessity for radical denazification were stilled by Buchenwald and Auschwitz."[14]

Even so, some policymakers and Army officials were doubtful of this policy. Before the war's end, the Combined Civil Affairs Committee, organized by the British and American armies, had developed political, economic, financial, and relief guides, which were "remarkably moderate."[15] Moreover, after the war's end, George Kennan wrote that denazification was unnecessary and impossible. Surveys, done by Army personnel, of prisoners of war and the occupied population lent some support to this perspective. The Army found little support for Nazism and an even stronger hatred of the Wehrmacht. The ruinous war had already done much to make the occupation authorities' job easier.[16]

Nevertheless, early policy was certainly not forgiving. In August 1945, the occupation authority's chief regulating document, JCS 1067, stated that all Nazi party members were to be forced from all public office.[17] The American theory of collective guilt led to a less nuanced approach to the German population and a more expansive denazification policy. Harold Zink offers the following comparison of the four occupying powers:

> The British certainly had a more professional attitude gained from their long experience with colonial peoples, but displayed less sentimental concern for German suffering. The Russians and French followed a distinctly hard course as far as the Germans in general were concerned. They lived off the country in contrast to the American and British policy of feeding their forces from imported stocks. They did not hesitate to liquidate Germans whom they regarded as inimical. But . . . they saw fit to extend a high degree of cordiality and favor to those Germans whom they regarded as important to their future interests.[18]

At the end of 1945, Lucius Clay announced that the American authorities had interned 100,000 Nazis. The British reported 64,000 in prison; the Soviets 67,000; and the French 19,000.[19]

Despite these incarcerations, the beginning of the American denazification campaign was hampered by massive confusion. It was not until July 1945 that the central command issued a uniform policy, which no tactical unit could change. It is doubtful, however, that this intervention clarified matters, since this document "created 136 categories under which removal from any kind of public service was mandatory."[20] Clay, however, was to add to the growing bewilderment by asserting that all Nazis should also be driven out of industry. On September 26, Law No. 8 was issued and declared that: "It shall be unlawful for any business enterprise to employ any member of the Nazi Party or its affiliate organizations in any supervisory or managerial capacity, or otherwise than ordinary labor."[21]

Clay's determination to purge his zone of Nazi influence soon foundered on insuperable administrative difficulties. He had issued the law without checking with his own denazification staff, who consistently argued for a more focused attack on the "big shots" that would stay firmly in American hands. Instead: "Enforcement was to be handled by having each firm report to municipal labor offices, and MG [military government] was to spot-check these reports, a mammoth and quite impossible task."[22]

Given the extraordinarily chaotic personnel problems of 1945, the only possible way to implement Law No. 8 was to turn the matter over to dependable Germans. Thus, three-person committees were created on the local level to oversee the denazification process. Soon, however:

> Appeal boards were . . . swamped, yet an individual was not to be employed until his appeal was acted. Confusion persisted as to whether a person could be employed in the same enterprise by changing job titles, a widespread means of evasion. The law did not refer to the self-employed or to those who owned a business, only to employees. There was confusion as to whether the Nazis' property should be kept from them, and which division should enforce this. The worst feature of Law No. 8 was that it included so-called little Nazis, by forcing them into manual labor when their skills could

have been more productive elsewhere. . . . *The law was not seriously crippling only because it was not seriously implemented.*[23] (My emphasis)

Despite these difficulties, Clay remained committed to the dual goals of extensive denazification and the extremely quick transfer of authority to indigenous political elites. The result was the issuing of a harsh denazification statute during March 1946 that would be regulated by German tribunals.[24] It is this Law for the Liberation from National Socialism that led to the issuing of a questionnaire of *Fragebogen* to every German over the age of 18. Authorities distributed 12 million questionnaires, and the results of this survey starkly revealed the mass collaboration of Germans with Hitler's regime. This made the job of denazification even more daunting: "Some three million persons, it was discovered, would have to be brought to trial. Tribunals of politically clean amateurs had to be created to try one-fourth of the adult population."[25] Even these results understate the problem. The Fragebogen had revealed that 29 percent of the adult population had been Nazi Party members; that 60 percent of the population had family members who were Nazis; and that wealthy Germans, even if they had Nazi sympathies, often did not join the National Socialists. The actual officials of Hitler's regime were more likely to be poorer people who were dependent on their job as their only source of income.[26]

Given this reality, it is not surprising that members of the German tribunals did not share Clay's passion for a complete purge of their own society. Clay criticized the failure of his German subjects to take denazification seriously on November 5, 1946. He threatened that if Germans did not seriously implement the Law for the Liberation from National Socialism, the military government would "necessarily have to take measures to see that denazification is carried out."[27] Despite this declaration, some of his own staff suspected that Clay himself did not wish to allow the American staff to pursue Nazis aggressively. His own personal advisor left because Clay refused to make changes in the law that would have allowed the military government to focus its efforts, and another staff officer wrote later that it was impossible to supervise the actions of the German tribunals. "No statistical reporting system was ever really set up and higher supervising MG levels had only the vaguest idea of what was actually happening in the field."[28]

Clay's paradoxical inability to implement an effective denazification policy was due to his overriding commitment to shrinking his governing staff as quickly as possible. His own reminiscences of this period and the many memoranda he sent to Washington suggest that the prosaic problem of cost cutting was always uppermost in his mind. The chaotic environment immediately after the war meant that American officials had to determine a way to hand over Germany to acceptable political elites as soon as possible. Thus, despite Clay's apparent commitment to denazification, he pursued an administrative strategy that undermined his own policy. Two months after his threat to place the denazification back in American control: "Matters reverted to where they had been, as it became clear that Clay could not carry out his threat to resume direct MG operations. Classification became consistently more lenient."[29] The imperative to withdraw from the direct governing of society overwhelmed almost all other efforts to reshape Germany.

It is for this reason that "democratization" developed at such a rapid pace in the American Zone. During the fall of 1945, Clay pushed for rapid delegation of authority to German officials by ordering that: "Local detachments were no longer to command German authorities, but merely to observe and to report delinquencies to higher headquarters."[30] This was pushed forward despite the fact that Americans had less contact with local German politicians than any of the other occupation authorities and thus were not in a position to be competent observers.

Nevertheless, Clay quickly created the institutions that would force American military government to withdraw by ordering local elections for villages to take place in January 1946, even though advisors in the State and War Departments objected to the speed of Clay's democratization plans.[31] It was in the rural areas that the Americans had the least ability to exercise control, and Clay apparently wanted to see whether it would be safe to hold local elections in more strategically sensitive and politically visible areas of the Zone. The explanation for this action is straightforward and is provided by Clay himself in a letter to John McCloy: "With so many officers returning to the U.S. during the coming months, we will certainly not be able to staff a large number of the local detachments with qualified men even by a vigorous recruiting program. Yet, we can hardly withdraw the local detachments until the officials appointed by us have been replaced by others selected by the Germans."[32]

The success of this exercise led to further elections for the "counties" and cities in early 1946.[33] Much to many observers' surprise, it was relatively easy to reconstitute a German political system willing and able to cooperate with the British and American authorities. Even statements from Communist Party leaders issued shortly after VE Day suggest that many activists were eager to participate in a parliamentary polity that permitted the functioning of a largely market-oriented, capitalist economic system. The results of the Army's surveys combined with those of the denazification questionnaires tell us that Germans who had passively supported or not bothered Hitler's regime were eager to return to a more "normal" political system. As Hannah Arendt might have said, the evil of Nazism reached deep into German society—just as it did in the white American South or white South Africa—but so did the banal desire of many individual Germans to embrace the cozy bourgeois politics of patronage and cautious social experimentation.

The aggressive plans to teach all the German people a lesson died early. Political restructuring did not require many positive decisions from the military government. Clay's decision to turn over authority as rapidly as possible and his inability to contest lax denazification decisions made by the new German authorities permitted a rapid evolution toward self-rule. The insuperable administrative barriers created by Clay's very aggressive vision of a wholesale purging of German society soon gave way to his even stronger determination to remove American personnel from the direct governing of German society. The realities of growing administrative powerlessness imposed by the movement of large numbers of qualified soldiers back home to America left Clay with little choice. America's successful political restructuring of West German society really amounted to little more than the handing over of the reins of power to acceptable political elites already eager to ally themselves with Western interests.

America's First Economic Policy toward Germany: The Development of the Hard Potsdam Peace

Economic reconstruction proved to be much more difficult than political reconstruction. Before the war's end, the Americans anticipated taking aggressive actions to reorganize the structures of the German polity and economy while doing nothing to support the living standards of the German people—who were assumed to be capable of supporting themselves.[34] In fact, American calculations were wrong on both counts. German political activists were eager to reorganize the polity without interference, while the economy required both massive quantities of food aid *and* the reconstruction of institutions that would both permit unhindered internal trade and allow Germany to trade with the rest of the world.

As the Army's pamphlet for occupying soldiers suggested, the American perspective derived less from the immediate experience of World War II and its attendant economic difficulties and more from the financial debacles of the post–Versailles 1920s. The obsession to avoid any financial commitments stemmed from a particular reading of both the Versailles Treaty's failures and the financial instability of the interwar period. American officials understood during World War II that reparations would once again be a key feature of a postwar settlement. On the other hand, analysts well remembered the failure of France to collect German reparations during the 1920s, the inability of any power to prevent the remilitarization of Germany, and the inability of the United States to protect its banks from defaults on the loans that had been extended, at least in part, to finance reparation payments.

One conclusion drawn from this interwar fiasco was that the Versailles Treaty's enforcement mechanisms were *too lenient.* U.S. government analysts believed that the Allies had failed to exercise sufficient controls over Weimar Germany and thereby allowed successive governments to subvert the intentions of the victors. As Henry Fowler, Director of the Enemy Branch of the Foreign Economic Administration (and future Secretary of the Treasury under Lyndon Johnson) put it:

The most important fact about Germany today is the size and the range of the existing industrial plant. It has been geared for total war and can be geared again; the bone, muscle and sinew of the economic and industrial war power that nearly conquered the world is still in existence—Germany's economic base for aggression remains to be eliminated or put under long-term control. . . . It serves no useful purpose to enter upon a program that bravely restricts a defeated Germany in 1946, but expires into feeble and impractical ineffectiveness in 1956 or 1976.[35]

Given these particular concerns, the problem of devising appropriate mechanisms for both the extraction of reparations and the limitation of future German economic power was of major concern to postwar planners. One solution was to specify a physical quantity of reparations deliveries, which would have to be supplied by Germany to the victorious powers. This demonetization of reparations, it was thought, would make it more difficult for Germany to borrow money in order to avoid or postpone paying reparations out of either current production or the existing stock of capital assets.[36]

The Potsdam agreement stressed the importance of administrative unification, but created a schizophrenic political economic framework to meet the immediate Soviet demand for German reparations. All of the Allies agreed to the eventual creation of a *unified* trading system, which would give priority to the use of export proceeds for the importation of essential commodities. On the other hand, the agreement allowed the Soviets to get the bulk of their reparations out of the capital stock of their own zone, while promising the delivery of 25 percent of the "surplus capital" of the Western zone to the Russians.[37] Secretary of State James Byrnes' explanation of this decision is pragmatic:

We knew that if reparations were to be drawn from all Germany we would have to demand an accounting from the Soviets. We were sure they could not even approximate an accurate valuation of what had been taken, and we realized that the effort to establish and maintain such an accounting would be a source of constant friction, accusations and ill-will.[38]

The amount that the Soviets would actually extract from Germany was purposefully left obscure. The four powers would determine the amount of surplus available in the West by listing the capital assets that would not be needed to provide the German people with a minimal, but self-sufficient, standard of living. This conclusion represented a clear American victory. Alec Cairncross, however, pithily underlined the pyrrhic nature of this triumph. He quipped that the argument in favor of payment in kind or through labor services by "workers detained in the receiving country" meant "loot and slavery, the traditional forms of reparations, had returned to favor."[39]

Given the unbelievable scale and nature of Nazi atrocities, not many were moved by this moral issue in 1945. Nevertheless, there were good practical reasons to be skeptical of the workability of the Potsdam agreement. Reaching a decision on how to negotiate the complicated mechanisms for a self-sufficient Germany is not the same as actually achieving this goal. It was not at all clear that President Truman and Secretary of State Byrnes had achieved their "overriding goal" of clearing up the "remaining military and economic responsibilities in Europe . . . as quickly as possible."[40] In fact, President Truman was on very weak ground when he reported to the American people that an important achievement of the Big Three summit was the adoption of the formula for reparations which would permit the United States government to avoid any financial commitments to Germany.[41]

The Economic Conditions and Financial Constraints Facing the OMGUS Economic Team

The Army officers who made up the American economic team in Berlin faced a daunting task. The Potsdam agreement required the officers to rigorously control German trade and develop a detailed economic plan. Instead, economic conditions were so grim that the economic team was forced to advocate policies that would promote economic revival rather than control.

The breakdown of the German economy was plain to see for all who visited Germany. It is useful to quote one early OMGUS report at length:

> Upon U.S. Military Government becoming operational in Berlin in July 1945 an industrial survey was conducted by this Headquarters and established the fact, that large industry, namely plants employing 25 persons or more, had a potential of 2% of normal capacity. This extremely low figure was a result of damage caused by bombing and artillery fire, plus the fact, that certain allied forces had removed a large percentage of equipment and raw materials. During the past few months there has been a tendency on the part of civilian industrialists to improve this situation by obtaining some equipment from unknown sources and by rebuilding machinery through the method of cannibalization. It would be safe to assume that there has been an increase in the industrial potential to about 6% of normal.[42]

Given these conditions, the prospects for establishing a self-sufficient trade regime in which export revenues paid for imports seemed very dim to OMGUS administrators during the first year and a half of their "rule." Between May and October 1945, the United States imported goods into the American Zone that were three times the value of German exports. During 1946, the trade gap grew even larger. Export revenues could pay for less than one-tenth of the American zone's imports.[43]

The imbalances, however, were not just due to war devastation. Because of the division of Germany into four separate zones of occupation and because of the demand for compensation by governments of countries once occupied by the Nazis, the transaction costs associated with reestablishing normal international trade relations were very high. Indeed, seven months after VE Day, the procedures used to pay for imports were apparently unknown to key American economic officials charged with monitoring German commerce. On December 6, 1945, Frederick Winant, Director of the Trade and Commerce Branch of the Economic Division headquarters, called the Assistant Executive of the Economics Division to inquire how to pay for Danish seed. As the weekly report puts it:

Mr. Winant requested that this Office find out:

(1) Who was [*sic*] authority to commit the U.S. to pay dollar exchange in connection with contract?

(2) "How do we follow up and actually pay for the seed when they [*sic*] reach the Danish border—i.e., what is the procedure?"[44]

This question required a detailed response from Colonel Frank T. Balke of the Trade and Commerce Branch. His answer was far from encouraging to those who wished to stimulate more normal commercial relations.

What seems required is a request, signed by Director, Office of Military Government for Germany (U.S.) to Commanding General, U.S. Forces, European Theater, Attn: G-4, Plans and Procedures Branch, asking that Commanding General, Theater Service Forces, European Theater, Attn: Procurement and Reciprocal Aid Section, negotiate the purchase, on U.S. Army account, of a designated quantity of seed for dollar exchange. Under the procedure worked by Lt. Col. Sawyer, until recently Quartermaster procurement agent in Denmark, the Danish government itself purchases the commodities from the private Danish suppliers; the U.S. representative then buys from the Danish government by giving it a U.S. Army purchase order form setting up a dollar credit at the Federal Reserve Bank, New York. This credit is in a "post-War Account", and the conditions governing its use are, of course prescribed by the U.S. Treasury.[45]

Even more aggravating than the difficulty of restarting commercially oriented international trade was the breakdown of internal trade in Germany. The documents on this subject within military government in Berlin reveal the constant frustrations that administrators faced. For example, in August 1945, Colonel Maurice Scharff of the Industry Division wrote to the Director of Trade and Commerce to note: "This problem of opening commercial channels for procurement of production material is becoming increasingly pressing as an obstacle to meeting requirements for military and minimum essential civilian use. It is urgently requested that action to find a solution to the problem be pressed in every possible way."[46] This message was part of a cover letter in which Scharff outlined the difficulties of interzonal transfers in more detail to Army authorities in charge of the tactical units. "No channel for commercial interzonal transfers is available; and . . . the only method of transfer officially authorized in this interim period is that required for military or minimum essential civilian use and arranged between the HQ Command of one Zone and the HQ Command of another Zone. It may further be pointed as a practical consideration that no facilities are available here in Berlin for clearing any questions relating to interzonal transfers with the representatives of the other occupying powers on the Quadripartite and Control Council staff."[47]

The frustrations with this cumbersome method of trade control led to a series of grassroots attempts to develop a regime of freer trade. One memorandum on November 10, 1945, revealed that Americans were advocating the same process of withdrawal that was used to "reform" German politics. The issue was to develop a trade of fattened cattle for breeding cattle between the two zones. Given the great shortages of slaughter cattle as well as of feed, the American officer "in charge" of this trade argued that: "The best thing we can do right now, would be to turn this project to the German livestock associations in the British and American Zones and let them decide if they want to trade—as they know the facts of each Zone."[48] Given the basic similarity in the goals of the British and American authorities—to construct a market economy and to reduce financial obligations as much as possible—the administrators in these two zones were able to use the strategy of retreating from controls in order to stimulate trade.[49]

The attempt to establish commercially oriented trading relations between the Soviet Zone and Western zones was far more problematic. On September 8, 1945, American officials complained of the continuing failure of the Russians to attend Economic Directorate meetings and keep appointments:

At a regularly called meeting of the Electricity and Gas Committee, on 3 Sept. the Russian representative failed to appear, without any advance notice to the other members. At an important meeting of the Industry Committee to discuss advance deliveries on reparations, the regular representative did not appear as he was out of the city and his alternate did not seem to be either as well informed or provided with as much authority as the regular representative. After an appointment had been made with the Russian representative on the Industry Committee several days in advance of the time when it was stated he would have returned, the U.S. representative went to the appointment and was informed that the Russian representative had not yet returned, although no prior notice had been given. Since the distance to the Russian headquarters is about 15 miles and since 30 to 60 minutes are usually required to secure telephone clearance on arrival at the Liaison Office, these difficulties are causing considerable loss of time.[50]

It is clear that this was not just a bad week for the U.S. representatives. Three months later, S. G. Wennberg of the Economics Division sent a memorandum to his chief, General William Draper, in which he stated:"The failure of the Soviet Delegate to appear at the meeting today [of the Central German Administrative Departments Committee] is the latest development in what appears to be a deliberate attempt on the part of the Soviet Delegation to delay the work of the Committee. Although it was agreed, back in September, to establish a Working Party to consider establishment of a Central German Administrative Department for Foreign Trade, no meeting of this Working Party has been held."[51]

As of January 9, 1946, quadripartite authorities still had not agreed on their "lily-white" list of goods that could be traded without controls. In the face of this intransigence, the Americans could only: "Check with the Military Government Authorities in the French and Russian Zones . . . to determine to what extent . . . action may be expected from them."[52]

Thus, the American team of economic advisors soon found themselves pursuing a two-track policy. On the one hand, the Potsdam agreement required the Economics Division to pursue negotiations that could establish German-staffed administrative organizations to organize exports and ration essential goods that needed to be imported in accordance with an agreed-upon plan. On the other hand, the press of daily events led the American team to take unilateral actions which in practice separated the economic activity of the American and British Zones from that of the Soviets. It is clear from the documents of the period that most, if not all, of the staff working on the OMGUS economic team preferred working on the more unilateral projects which might prove to be more successful.[53] The conclusion the American officials took from this experience was that it was essential to construct a more stable economic structure that could *remove* Americans from direct administrative responsibilities.

The Failed Attempt to Implement the Potsdam Accord

Despite these basic political economic difficulties, Lucius Clay believed that the key task necessary for the construction of a unified, self-sufficient German economy was the negotiation of a level of industry agreement. If the Allies could agree on the structure and magnitude of German economic activity during the early postwar years, this might lead to the implementation of a reparations plan, demilitarization plan, and trade plan. First, a level of industry agreement would allow the allied economists to identify the surplus capital equipment that could be shipped to the victims of Nazi occupation. Second, the schedule for removals would allow the Allies to dismantle the so-called military-related industry that had permitted Germany to wage two world wars. Third, the plan would permit enough capital equipment to remain that the German economy could be self-supporting; i.e., export revenues would be able to pay for necessary imports and the population would not starve. The chief economic officer of OMGUS (and Clay's second in command), William Draper, reflected on American efforts some two years after this first attempt. "If it had turned out that the level of industry was the key, and that once that had been agreed. . . . the rest of it would be comparatively easy [*sic*]. If, following that, we had been able to reach agreement on treating Germany as an economic whole, to install the administrative German agencies, turn over the job at that time so far as the operation was concerned to the Germans under Allied supervision, and if the resources of all four zones had been made available on an equal basis to all four zones through all of Germany, a great many of the problems that have developed since would have been avoided."[54]

Draper and the Americans obsessively focused on reaching a level of industry agreement because they unrealistically believed that it might be possible to withdraw American financial support for the German economy if the Allies could economically unify the occupied zones. Once the commitment to these negotiations was made, it was clearly necessary to assemble a staff of economists who could provide the calculations necessary for the construction of a reasonable plan. The work came in three stages: to determine the appropriate economic level and structure of a demilitarized postwar Germany; to calculate the export and import requirements necessary to guarantee German self-sufficiency; and to identify the "surplus" capital equipment which could be turned over for distribution to the Allied Reparations Board. All of this technical work supported a negotiation process among the Military Governors or Deputy Military Governors of France, the UK, the USSR, and the USA, and was meant to prepare the ground for the complete integration of the German economy and a reduction in the American financial commitment to a prostrate Germany.[55]

In order to compromise with the Soviet Union and an equally vengeful France, the Americans picked a production level that could only have perpetuated the impoverishment of the immediate postwar years. On September 17, 1945, the United States authorities submitted a study entitled "A Minimum German Standard of Living in Relation to the Level of Industry" to the Level of Industry Committee of the Allied Control Authority's Directorate of Economics. This report (the production of which was supervised by Professor Calvin Hoover from Duke University), took the *per capita* European average (excluding Britain and the Soviet Union) income level between 1930 and 1938 as the target the German economy should attain within the next few years. Since Germany's production was considerably above that of its European neighbors during the 1930s, the study argued that Germany's industry and agricultural capacity should only permit levels of activity similar to those attained during 1932.

The authors of the report did not note the ironic political implications of picking 1932 for a German production standard. The German economy was then in the very depths of the Depression.

The devastating economic conditions of that time were a major reason for Hitler's ascendancy the following year. "A Minimum German Standard of Living" (or the Hoover Report), however, did focus on the difficulty of maintaining an import and export balance under such circumstances. The report estimated that the loss of the vast agricultural lands of East Prussia to Poland and Russia, as well as the dismantling of key industries such as ocean shipping, airplanes, aluminum, ammonia, and magnesium, would lead Germany to run a 161 million Reich mark trade deficit, even before counting the 2.7 billion Reich mark occupation costs the German economy was expected to bear.[56]

Partly because of these imbalances, the American negotiating team allowed the negotiation process to cut German imports more deeply. On January 28, 1946, Draper presented a new and revised version of "The Future Level of the German Standard of Living" to the Allied Control Authority. This document represented a fuller specification of the earlier September report. The new submission no longer mentioned 1932 production levels as the appropriate target, but instead called for a 25 or 30 percent *cut* in production from 1936 levels as the appropriate output target for Germany in 1949.[57]

The American economic team produced this second edition of the level of industry plan in response to the often acrimonious negotiations that took place throughout the late autumn and early winter. Given the conflicting claims and intense time pressure, it was inevitable that the negotiation process was chaotic. Alec Cairncross summarizes the results well when he writes: "The haggling over steel was typical of the way in which negotiations between the four powers were conducted. Levels for other industries were fixed in a bargaining process without any attempt to investigate the repercussions on other industries and so check that exports would still have a reasonable chance of balancing imports. . . . No set of figures less resembled a plan than the hotchpotch resulting from the Dutch auction in Berlin."[58]

The chief American negotiator drew similar conclusions in a more personal way. B. U. Ratchford, Hoover's replacement as Chief Economic Advisor of the Level of Industry Committee, captures best the tense and troubled experience of the negotiations when he writes in the third person about himself: "Ratchford . . . had no official coaching or instruction whatever in policy matters. He had to learn about, or guess at, U.S. policy as best he could with no time to consider it carefully. On many occasions he had to take a position "off the cuff" without benefit of any previous reflection, advice, or instruction. In many respects he felt like a man who had suddenly been promoted from Captain to Brigadier General and thrust out on the firing line with no troops under him and no liaison or supply lines to the rear."[59] This excitement could not mask his unease at the results. After a particularly crucial meeting that set heavy equipment and automobile levels, Ratchford and his co-author write: "The meeting was over. Decisions had been made that would affect the lives of millions of people—decisions that represented millions of dollars. Is history made so haphazardly, so unscientifically?"[60]

There was good reason for this unhappiness. The negotiating process had resolved very little. There was little consensus over the meaning of the documents. The Soviets and French thought of them as establishing permanent production ceilings, while the Americans and British argued that the documents established a mechanism for determining how much surplus equipment could be removed as reparations. Once this resource extraction process was completed, the Anglo-American perspective foresaw the construction of new equipment as part of Germany's reconstruction process. Thus, one side viewed the "hotchpotch" as a plan, while the other viewed it as a document that would determine the appropriate size of reparation payments. Neither perspective was particularly plausible, especially since there was little agreement in the document on the capacity necessary to produce the minimum or maximum production levels.[61]

On March 28, 1946, the British, French, Soviet, and American Military Governors announced the Allied agreement to *The Plan for Reparations and the Level of Post-War Germany Economy in Accordance with the Berlin Protocol*. The agreement cut imports even further and placed stricter limits on German steel production than American and British negotiators desired. Despite these problems, Ratchford and Ross proudly state, "an historic document was written."[62] In retrospect, however, all the early postwar efforts to negotiate Germany's future are historical muddles and curiosities—more like discarded furniture in an attic. The negotiators themselves had grave disputes over the substance of the agreement, and no one seemed to have considered the mechanics of either administratively unifying the German economy or completing the dismantling of complicated capital equipment within two years. These problems proved to be insuperable.

By spring 1946, clear choices faced the Soviet and American governments. The Allied Control Council had finally negotiated a level of industry agreement, and now it was time, according to American plans, to construct a unified trading administration for all of Germany. For one month after the March 1946 agreement to the level of industry plan, General Clay attempted to negotiate the creation of central administrative agencies for the whole of Germany. During this frustrating process, Clay restated the American position that the level of industry agreement had made reparations, and export-import balance interdependent. "When [Soviet General Mikhail] Dratvin denied the relationship between reparations and export-imports, Clay announced that because none of the main economic provisions of Potsdam had been executed, the United States would stop dismantling German industry."[63]

The Soviets, in turn, retaliated during the following month by announcing officially the creation of Soviet-German companies which could deliver a substantial proportion of output to the Soviet Union as reparations.[64] Within five weeks of the negotiation of this "historic" level of industry document, the agreement was in shambles. At this point serious efforts to unify Germany economically ceased.

The Local Resistance to Potsdam

This breakdown of the Potsdam economic negotiations is one of the more curious episodes of the immediate postwar period. Lucius Clay apparently made the decision to withhold American reparation deliveries without consulting Washington. Until this time, the General was one of the most enthusiastic proponents of the quadripartite economic negotiations. He was one of the last to question the basic premise of the harsh Potsdam Accord, and he believed well into late 1946 that a Soviet-American deal over Germany was possible.

One explanation of this rather abrupt about-face must lie farther down the chain of command. There were very few members of the economic staff in Berlin who supported the Potsdam negotiations with any enthusiasm. The difficult economic and financial conditions described in the previous section had made the professional staff very skeptical of any negotiating process that discussed limited German reconstruction at a time when economic activity was far below what even the harshest critic of German society would consider as acceptable.

The Berlin-based economists' unhappiness with the results of their own work is manifested in several documents of this era. The difficulty in imagining a long-term plan that would both limit German production and permit economic self-sufficiency had confirmed many of the worst fears that OMGUS administrators in Germany had about the Potsdam Accord. U.S. economic officers working in the Industry Branch of the Economic Division were especially distressed by the mid-September submission of the standard of living plan to the Allied Directorate. On October 20, 1945, Colonel James Boyd, Chief of the Industry Branch, submitted a report to William Draper entitled "Report on Industrial Disarmament."[65] Every branch chief responsible for supervising a particular industrial sector in the American Zone endorsed the contents of the memo, which urged a significant modification in U.S. policy.

Boyd recognized the unusual nature of this protest in his covering letter when he wrote: "I realize that General Clay desires that modifications of U.S. policy should not originate from the Zone. However, the Section Chiefs of this Branch have all urged me to request their views be submitted in this form to the authorities who are making U.S. policy, and have asked that they be permitted to sign the report individually. I am submitting it to you as the view of the Branch."[66]

The "Report on Industrial Disarmament" was also known as the Leighton report, because Captain Bruce Leighton coordinated its writing before leaving for the States. The memo basically argued for a narrow interpretation of the Potsdam agreement. Leighton granted that the American government was obligated to dismantle all military production facilities, but then suggested that: "Authoritative agencies all agree that in modern total war nearly *all* industries are used for military production. The question now at issue is: How far, under the Potsdam agreement, is it necessary or desirable to carry Industrial Disarmament, beyond the mandatory elimination of military industrial facilities?"[67]

Leighton argued for a minimal dismantling process because of the "inescapable impact of significant changes in the economy of the German people upon the economy of Europe as a whole." The main long-term argument focused on the importance of maintaining Germany as a "solvent export [market] of 70 million consumers." This, in turn, suggested that there should not be any arbitrary efforts to limit the production of commodities that were not directly and solely related to wartime production.[68]

The report was certainly not a laissez-faire document. It endorsed efforts to limit steel and nonferrous metal production and trade. Moreover, the Leighton report rather surprisingly advocated the elimination of a heavy machine tool industry.[69] Nevertheless, the whole thrust of the Industrial Branch's argument was that OMGUS should take unilateral actions to revive industry in its zone. For this reason, the Leighton report sharply attacked the 1932 industrial standard that the Standard of Living Report had set, and, in fact, cast doubt on the exercise of setting a standard of living on the basis of past economic historical experience.[70]

This internal memorandum from Berlin strongly resembles the arguments of State Department economists such as Charles Kindleberger. It is not likely that the economic staff in Berlin knew of this higher-level support of their perspectives. Nor is there much evidence that Clay paid attention to the soft peace advocates in Washington. That is why the Leighton report is so significant. The opposition of Clay's economic officers to the policy which they were working so hard to implement had little initial effect on Lucius Clay's drive to reach some sort of accommodation with the Soviets. The General did not seem to realize that the Russians would never agree to a plan that could not guarantee substantial reparation deliveries. When the Soviets definitively rejected the American interpretation of the level of industry plan, however, the disappointed Clay embraced the thinking of his economic advisors without any apparent reservation. From May 1946 on, there was no high policy official in the United States government who was a more effective advocate for Germany's economic revival than Lucius Clay.

The Leighton report had prepared the way for this almost seamless rejection of the Potsdam framework. Just as with the process of political reform, the American efforts to control German economic life directly collapsed. Instead, Army officers eagerly strove to divest themselves of direct responsibility for managing the Germany economy. Unlike the efforts to reform the political realm, Clay followed the thinking of his junior staff rather than leading it. In this case, growing geopolitical tension intersected with continued economic chaos to force a change of policy in the higher level officers. The junior officers recognized the need for a shift of focus before General Clay did. The result, however, was the same. The inability of the Army to control political and economic events in Germany permitted the relatively rapid emergence of a partnership with German political elites in the British and American zones of occupation.

Chapter V

Between Boot Camp and Summer Camp

The withdrawal of American officials from the direct regulation of German political and economic life permitted Army officers to focus more single-mindedly on the morale and discipline problems plaguing the occupation army. Through 1946 and 1947, the Army introduced a series of measures that can be best described as a carrot-stick approach to regulating GI behavior. On the one hand, the Army drew on its successful British "occupation" experience and provided "wholesome" educational and recreational outlets. On the other hand, the Army created a rather fearsome American constabulary under the aggressive leadership of tank commander General Ernest Harmon to supervise and control the American and German populations in the occupation zones.

A close reading of the documents of this period suggests that the lenient approach had more success than harsh disciplinary measures. It took time, however, for the Army to discover the correct proportions of discipline and benefits. Eventually, it is this army of comfortable martial tourists that became the backbone of the Cold War army.

Early Missteps

Disciplined training, indoctrination, education, tourism, sports, and general entertainment were the key aspects of the Army's efforts to strengthen the occupation army. Beyond this general list, however, the approach of the Army to the problem of worker morale cannot be summarized easily. Different commanders chose different mixes of drills, training programs, and entertainment. On the one hand, the Army did not wish to impose regimens of discipline that would be so unpopular they would be difficult to enforce. The fraternization ban fiasco had taught officers in Germany that it was necessary to accommodate some rank and file desires. On the other hand, no general could sanguinely contemplate the erosion of military command—especially as the behavior of American troops was becoming a political liability in the United States.

The problem of finding the right balance of accommodation is exemplified by the minor controversy that surrounds Dwight Eisenhower's lenient approach to the ordinary GI during the latter half of 1945. Despite the clear evidence of disciplinary problems associated with the excess consumption of liquor and black marketing, the European Theater command decided during September 1945 to increase the amount of liquor available to soldiers and to permit the selling of surplus goods (including automobiles) to the American troops.[1] These decisions solidified Eisenhower's reputation as a politically astute general who cared about the welfare of his troops.

Other generals, however, believed that he was too lenient and made the job more difficult for other commanding officers. The Commanding General of the American Constabulary, Ernest Harmon, writes:

At this time [January 1946] the discipline of the Army in Europe was at very low ebb. That is all anybody talked about. I think General Eisenhower made a mistake in not putting the men to work in the mornings as General Pershing had done in World War I. The soldiers without much adieu got into a lot of mischief. Most of my trouble came from the American soldier; almost none at all came from the German population. . . .

This leads me to the philosophical statement that U.S.O. shows, doughnuts, and all these thing [sic] that are very nice to have, slack and easy discipline, is not what makes people proud. People are proud to belong to something that requires to put forth their best effort. . . ."[2]

Although inelegantly and ungrammatically phrased, Harmon's "philosophical statement" gets to the core of the dilemma facing officers involved in the occupation of Germany. How much emphasis should be placed on discipline and work projects, and how many resources should be devoted to leisure activities that could range from general education to theater productions to athletics to tourism? Should the Army in Germany resemble a gigantic boot camp or should the occupation Army turn into something like a huge network of year-round summer camps which could promise both educational improvement and desexualized entertainment?

General Harmon chose to emphasize discipline as opposed to entertainment because he commanded the newly formed Constabulary, the only unit in Germany which had a clear daily mission: to preserve order within the American Zone. This motorized police force required an extensive training program since few soldiers had any real background in police work. Harmon also believed that it was necessary to establish a clear esprit de corps by establishing new uniforms and personally inspecting every constabulary unit at least once every month. His constant inspection trips in Hermann Goering's old personal train inspired fear and grudging respect among all the officers under his command.

General Harmon's techniques placed the ordinary Constabulary soldier under more constraints than his brethren in the Third Army. For example, all members of the Constabulary force were strictly forbidden from writing in complaints to the popular Army newspaper *Stars and Stripes*. Harmon personally expelled from the force the first soldier who had a letter published in the B-Bag column of this newspaper. Despite the controversy, Harmon could count on the backing of Eisenhower's replacement, General Joseph McNarney, who also launched a campaign to improve standards of military courtesy and bearing within all the military forces.[3]

Despite the shift to a harsher regimen, it is doubtful that there was much positive effect on the activity of the ordinary soldier. Chapter I has already documented the rising crime rate that plagued the American Army throughout 1946. Perhaps even more striking is the inability of Harmon's vigorous command to prevent the same problems within the Constabulary itself. The March 1947 *Statistical Report of Operations,* for example, notes that the Constabulary soldiers were responsible for 126 of the 342 "Crimes, Offenses and Serious Incidents" of that month. The data indicate that the soldiers of the police force were especially involved in assaults and larceny.[4] Nor were the March 1947 data an aberration. In fact, the crime rate among Constabulary personnel rose from 1.20 incidents per 1,000 soldiers per month in July 1946 to 3.68 per 1,000 in June 1947. Throughout this period: "The rate of serious incidents involving Constabulary troops was somewhat higher than that of other troops in the theater."[5]

Problems within the Constabulary reflected a more general difficulty in controlling those members of the Army whose duties permitted them to travel throughout the occupation zone away from direct supervision. No amount of inspections could overcome the temptations that motorized, militarized power offered.

The Failures of Indoctrination

This inability to rely on the law-abiding instincts of a sizeable minority of the Army suggests that it was difficult to convince the soldiers it was important to respect the property and personal security of their colleagues and of the subject population. During this early period of the occupation, the military never developed an effective orientation program to convince the ordinary soldiers that socially responsible behavior really mattered.

The initial indoctrination efforts probably had the opposite effect. Every soldier entering Germany during the final combat period and shortly after VE Day received the occupation booklet cited earlier. The soldiers were told: "Before the German people can learn how to govern themselves and get along with the rest of the world they must be firmly impressed with the fact that they have been defeated, that their acceptance of Nazi leadership made their defeat necessary and earned for them the distrust of free, peaceful people." The pamphlet enjoined the members of the entering Army:

1. To remember always that Germany, though conquered, is still a dangerous enemy.
2. Never to trust Germans, collectively or individually.
3. To defeat German efforts to poison [the soldiers'] thoughts or influence [their] attitude.[6]

Such rhetoric could obviously breed a general contempt for the German population, but it took more than a year before there was considerable change in the language that described the mission of the American occupation. It was only after Secretary of State Byrnes' September 1946 speech outlined a more benign American interest in German recovery that the Army changed its six-hour Troop Information Program to emphasize to the soldier "the positive aspects of the occupation, and to better acquaint him [the soldier] with his task and its [the occupation's] purpose. Built around the Stuttgart speech of former Secretary of State Byrnes, the program covers every phase of the occupation, including organization of the Theater, explanation of typical jobs of Military Government, the Military Police, the United States Constabulary, the Air Forces, the various service units, as well as the psychology of propaganda in its relation to German history."[7]

Despite this change, the orientation program had little effect. The final report of the Third Army complains that surveys revealed a considerable lack of interest in and knowledge about the Troop Information Program. The authors attribute this result to the "widespread failure to implement the program properly."[8] This focus on procedural failings was not new. As early as October 1945, General Eisenhower responded to the failings of the orientation program by doubling the amount of teaching time associated with this program to a compulsory four hours a week.[9] Approximately three months later, Secretary of War Robert Patterson visited the European Theater and reserved his harshest criticism for Information and Education officers. According to Patterson, the performance of instructors "was decidedly uneven" and "that it was necessary for all senior commanders to assure themselves that highly qualified officers are assigned to these duties.[10]

The image evoked by these documents is of a roomful of indifferent enlisted men listening to unenthusiastic officers lecture them about their mission in Germany. Unfortunately, abstract phrases such as "building democratic institutions" or "providing a good example of the American way of life" meant little to soldiers engaged in a boring round of meaningless drills. It became increasingly obvious to many soldiers that their main purpose in Germany was simply to be there. One might take pride in the importance of the United States that this symbolic presence indicated, and there is evidence that many soldiers did enjoy this reflected, geopolitical prestige. Still, dull lectures alone could not induce good behavior. No amount of discipline or orientation programs could keep a significant number of American soldiers under appropriate controls.

It was not clear if the Army had any solution at all to the problems of soldiers' unruliness. The Army Chaplains, for example, evidently believed that "the lack of smartness in appearance on the part of enlisted men in the army was due to (1) a lack of training in obedience at home, (2) the tenor of the age in refusing to recognize any lawful (Divine), military, or civil authority."[11]

Given this perception, the only solution seemed to lie in offering a variety of activities that might induce the soldier to engage in more responsible or less destructive activities. The following description of the Third Army's early 1946 programs summarizes this multi-faceted summer camp approach. "The Information-Education office was very active in the Headquarters area with its orientation and school programs. The athletic program was well advanced and went far toward providing well-balanced exercise accommodations for all men. The hour-a-day exercise schedule which was introduced in the quarter considerably stimulated participation in sports activities to which, with the construction of courts, squash and handball were added. There was considerable emphasis on the entertainment program and a variety of German floor shows and orchestras were secured for playing in the area."[12]

The Vagaries of the Army's Education Program

The Army's education program developed rapidly in response to the growing discontent of most soldiers, who wished to return to the United States as quickly as possible. The Army hoped that by offering courses, which would be useful to soldiers when they returned to civilian life, it might be possible to entice some soldiers to stay in Europe a while longer.

There is little evidence that this program actually weakened the desire of GIs to return to the United States. Nevertheless, the scale of the education program was impressive. By October 1945, the Third Army reported that nearly every battalion or regiment operated a command school. 660 instructors (75 percent enlisted men) taught 725 classes in 107 different subjects.[13] Most of these courses emphasized basic education, technical training, or art appreciation.[14]

Despite this rapid expansion, it proved impossible to maintain educational services at this scale. As early as December 1945, the number of soldiers attending courses throughout the European Theater declined by 36 percent, even though the number of courses increased from 146 to 221.[15] This reflected the rapid decline of the number of troops stationed in Germany between October 1945 and December 1945, the numbers in the Third Army dropped from 234,690 to 123,626.[16] Put in this context, the relative number of students attending classes actually increased. There was no weakening of the commitment to provide a wide-ranging educational pro-

Table 5.1   Schools in the Third Army   November 1945

Location	Subject	# students
Bad Tolz	Art	21
Freisung	Ag. & Sciences	694
Ansbach	Technical	171
Triesdorf	Agriculture	59
Kitzingen	Music	11
Oberammergan	Literacy Training	65
Bamberg	Art	50
Augsburg	High School	200
Bayreuth	High School	200
Regensburg	General Subjects	300

Source: G–3 Section, Headquarters, Third U.S. Army, "Report for the Month of November 1945" (Suitland, Md.: National Archives, Record Group 338, Box 67): 8–9.

gram. Indeed, despite the decline in the Army's number, the Third Army planned the establishment of an arts and crafts school by holding a course of study for potential instructors in Garmisch-Partenkirchen.[17] A skiing school in the same region followed in March 1946.[18] By the first quarter of 1946, approximately 3 percent of the army was involved in one course or another.[19]

Discrete programs went forward, but it was not possible to maintain the European Theater's Army University, which was briefly established in 1945 when Army planners anticipated a much larger army in Europe. Slowly the program became more rationalized with the closing of small unit command schools (which Information and Education officers considered ineffective), while retaining the larger schools, which were available to members of all units. The educational mission changed in order to focus on basic literacy training and technical courses that could be directly useful for the Army.[20] This shift, in turn, reflected the more pronounced working-class composition of the Army, as more formally educated servicemen eagerly returned home. By February 1946, enrollments had dropped by 50 percent.[21]

As the number of advanced courses in nontechnical subjects declined, the Army placed increasing emphasis on promoting lecture tours and establishing an impressive library and bookmobile system. During 1946's second quarter, there were as many as 31 librarians active in the Third Army area. They were responsible for keeping track of 24 bookmobiles and 195,566 books.[22] Meanwhile, a group of academic experts from the United Kingdom and other countries began to tour the Third Army region to give lectures that would "attempt to promote a better cultural and intellectual understanding of their respective countries."[23]

The arrival of wives and children in the European Theater briefly promised to increase enrollments, and, indeed, the number of students serviced in the Third Army area grew from 2,103 during the second quarter to 6,692 by the third quarter.[24] The extra cost of this expansion soon produced a reaction. The final quarter's report carried the complaint that: "A ruling that only military personnel may be enrolled in classes taught by United States Civilian instructors paid from War Department funds will no doubt cause a deep cut in overall attendance, as many dependents and Allied civilians have participated in the educational program. United States civilian employees may be enrolled in classes taught by instructors paid from other than War Department funds only when they can be accommodated without interfering with the enrollment of military personnel."[25]

It is interesting to note that by late 1946 the most popular course given by the Information and Education Section was German language study. (These began during June 1946, a full year after Germany's capitulation.[26]) The record suggests that all educational programs offered by the Army remained popular for a minority of soldiers throughout the occupation. Some took advantage of these programs in order to pursue higher education. Others developed cultural interests through what the Army offered, while still more took basic literacy classes and training courses in order to improve their career prospects inside and outside of the Army.

Tourism as Education and Entertainment

The early controversies over redeployment after VE Day had made it clear that it would be difficult to convince the typical soldier that it was useful for him to be in any occupied territory. The Army wasted no effort in persuading the troops that their presence was necessary. Evoking the sacrifice of the combat troops during World War II, an early orientation pamphlet opened by proclaiming: "You are here to protect a tremendous investment—to see that the swastika stays down. If it doesn't, those 150,000 American lives were wasted."[27]

If this exhortation was not completely convincing, travel and tourism served as a more positive inducement to serve. The soldier could be the stern protector of democracy and a tourist at the same time. The same pamphlet stated: "In a way, you can look on your tour of duty in occupied Germany as a chance to see some countries you might never had an opportunity to know outside the Army. Along with the primary jobs which you have ahead of you— selling democracy to the Nazis and controlling them until they really believe it—there are going to be chances for you to travel, regardless of the job you are doing."[28]

The early travel programs sponsored by the Army in Germany were extensive, but plagued by the same problem that the early education efforts were. The rapid reduction of troops in the European Theater led to a constant shuffling of the tours offered the soldiers on leave. The following two statements from the "Reports of Operations" of the last quarter of 1945 and the first quarter of 1946 summarize the fluidity of the tour program and the extensive logistical work required to organize tours.

> Early in the quarter, the Lourdes tour was terminated and the leave centers at Brussels and Luxembourg closed. On 22 December, however, a Swiss-Italian tour accommodating 200 persons per day was inaugurated in the Eastern Military District. This required a ten-day leave allowing four days in Switzerland and six in Italy. Also, in November, leave time for Paris was stepped up to seven days and that for Riviera and United Kingdom to ten days. The winter sports program gained momentum too, with the opening of a Winter Sports Tour to Val D'Isere, France.[29]
>
> A number of leave trains were discontinued during the quarter, among them being the Riviera leave train, the Paris- Kassel, Paris-Munich, and Nurnberg-Nice leave trains. Train service Paris-Nice was made available to Riviera leave personnel in military coaches on civilian trains, Paris to Nice. A dining car was placed in service between Munich and Salzburg on the Linz-Munich-Frankfurt duty train. To improve travel between Frankfurt and Linz, Austria, an all-military duty train was inaugurated between those two points with a sleeper section from Munich to Frankfurt.[30]

Cost was another issue facing the Army. As budgetary pressures grew, the European Theater decided in early 1946 to make all tours outside the occupation zones financially self-sufficient. The result of this new policy was that a USFET conference "drastically reduced" leave and furlough quotas allotted to the Third Army. By April 1, 1946, each soldier of the new occupation would receive two seven-day furloughs during each year. If they used an Army-sponsored tour, they would pay a flat rate. Enough facilities would exist so that 4 percent of the total Army personnel could be accommodated.[31]

Eventually, the American Express Company received the exclusive franchise to organize the tours outside the American Zone, and the Army's Special Services divisions served as the travel agent for soldiers booking such trips.[32] Families increasingly used these package tours in order to visit Czechoslovakia, Switzerland, Rome, Holland, Denmark, London, Paris, or the Riviera. American Express began offering discounted rates for children in order to encourage this family travel.[33] The impecunious students of the sixties were not the first bargain basement American tourists during the postwar era. Many of their older kin had already enjoyed the sights of Europe.

The shift to commercially organized package tours outside occupied Germany did not mean that the Army no longer ran facilities for recreating soldiers. In fact, the Army now focused on providing more opportunities for relaxation within the American Zone itself. For this purpose, the scenery that the United States acquired served the military well. The British may have possessed Germany's most extensive industrial and coal-mining area, and the Soviet Union may have enjoyed the food self-sufficiency which came from holding some of the Prussian agricultural territories, but neither of these occupation authorities could have put together recreational centers of such natural beauty. By late 1946, the Third Army had opened a hotel in Grumwald, Bavaria, and a mountain Rest Center in Garmisch-Partenkirchen.[34] Officers paid one dollar a day, while enlisted men handed over 50 cents in order to stay in these centers.[35] The evidence suggests that tours and more extended trips were enormously popular. During the second quarter of 1946 alone, 11,690 officers and enlisted men participated in organized tours throughout Bavaria.[36]

Recreation and Entertainment Closer to "Home": Sports, Movies, Theater, and Music

The organization of leisure activities did not just take place away from a soldier's workplace. Increasingly, the Army provided opportunities for the soldier to attend sporting events, movies, plays, and concerts. The majority of soldiers stayed in the audience, but such events also encouraged soldiers to develop their own athletic or artistic talents. It is clear that these activities stimulated broad interest and encouraged an esprit de corps among the American soldiers that might otherwise not have existed.

Sporting events especially encouraged soldiers to be loyal to their own units. As early as October 1945, commentators were writing of athletic activities as something that had been long and well established by the Third Army. "Sports continued to attract large numbers of participants and spectators and schedules were arranged to disperse events, particularly between Class A and Class B teams. The football season saw some excellent games, the basketball season got underway, and there was activity in shooting, soccer, swimming and other fields."[37] Interest was so great in inter–unit competitions that the American Armed Forces Network produced a daily sport show in January 1946 that covered the significant GI sporting events of the European Theater.[38]

The Third Army's "Report of Operations" began to report proudly on the accomplishments of its teams. The 1st Infantry Division's basketball team won the Class A Theater championships in early 1946, and the Adjutant General's section of Third Army Headquarters won the Class B competition.[39] Because of the competitive intensity and complaints of poor quality officiating, the Army even sponsored a series of special clinics for would-be referees or umpires.[40] One year after VE Day, soldiers in Germany were competing in volleyball, track and field, softball, horseshoes, golf, tennis, swimming and diving, and baseball.[41]

Despite the status of baseball as the "national pastime," football games attracted the largest number of GI fans. An amazing 60,000 supporters attended the opening day of the season on September 29, 1946. The commander of the Third Army, Lieutenant General Geoffrey Keyes, inaugurated the season by blowing the kick-off whistle for the competition between the Third U.S. Army Headquarters and the 47th Infantry Regiment.[42] Lasting until December 1, the season concluded extravagantly with three bowl games. "The 9th Infantry Division Special Troops played the 16th Infantry Regiment in the 'GI Rose Bowl'; the 39th Infantry Regiment and the Grafenwohr Military Community were 'GI Sugar Bowl' opponents; and the 1st Infantry Division Artillery met the 60th Infantry Regiment in the 'GI Orange Bowl' at Heidelberg."[43] The final championship game, between the 39th and 16th Infantry Regiments took place in December in Rotterdam before 30,000 Dutch spectators.[44] The endless cycle of sporting events so comforting to many American males began again in January 1947 with the launching of the basketball season. In this way, the Army replicated the familiar rhythms of the American sport year.

Another comforting feature of base life was cheap access to first-run American movies. During the last quarter of 1945, for example, 1.8 million soldiers saw approximately 6,200 showings of 35–millimeter films.[45] As Table 5.2 indicates, attendance remained high throughout the occupation, although some officers worried about certain releases, such as *The Maltese Falcon,* which seemed to promote a contempt for legally constituted authority. (For this reason, Army authorities only briefly allowed the German population to watch this film classic.)[46] Despite these reservations, the Army constructed large, 600–seat theaters in Stuttgart and Wurzburg and made the whole movie-showing operation financially self-supporting.[47]

Such enthusiasm for sports and the cinema will not surprise contemporary readers. What does seem different, however, is the Army's enthusiastic sponsorship of Soldier Theater. Throughout the first two years, surprisingly elaborate shows were developed, and many GI entertainers toured throughout the occupation zone. In October 1945, for example, the Third Army sponsored a Soldier Show Workshop which "was set up as an organization in which soldier shows will be staged, equipped and prepared for the road under the supervision of qualified theater technicians. As December ended, the pro-

Table 5.2   Movie Attendance During the First Quarter, 1946

	35 mm films		16 mm films	
	Showings	*Attendance*	*Showings*	*Attendance*
Jan.	1,860	70,640	1,712	465,748
Feb.	1,861	71,648	1,710	465,700
Mar.	1,872	74,281		

Source: "Report of Operations for the Period 1 January–31 March 1946," (Suitland. Md.: National Archives, Record Group 338, Box 67): 91.

ject was developing satisfactorily, having obtained more than thirty tons of costumes, scenery material, lighting mechanisms and such."[48]

It did not take long for the Army to organize an extensive program. By February 1946, four soldier shows were touring the Third Army. The most popular program was entitled "Script and Score" and played its 50th performance at Regensburg on February 21. During this short period, 25,000 soldiers attended this presentation.[49]

Professional tours organized by the USO also inundated the occupation zone. During late 1945, the Radio City Music Gala Revue attracted the largest number of GIs. In March 1946 alone, 105 USO-sponsored performances attracted a total audience of approximately 66,000. By May, the European Theater was even sponsoring a rodeo tour.[50]

Restructuring German–American Fraternization: Booze, Music, and German Youth Activities

Almost all of the entertainment and education activities outlined in this chapter concern the creation of structured events that involved American personnel alone. The hope was that such programs would reduce the more negative criminal and sexual activities that necessarily dominated the attention of military authorities. It was not possible or desirable to completely isolate the American soldier from the surrounding population, but it was necessary to limit the ability of soldiers to go on unsupervised rampages. Despite all the programs documented in this chapter, criminal activity was all too common as late as December 1946.

American authorities tried to such incidents by more aggressively restricting and observing the actions of off-duty American soldiers. Gone were the lenient days of General Eisenhower's post–VE Day command. Instead, the more repressive approach implemented by General McNarney required constant vigilance. M.P. patrols attempted to ensure that soldiers attended largely American-sponsored nightclubs and stayed away from German Kneipen. Between 11 P.M. and midnight, patrolling outside authorized clubs was especially intense, although it was not obvious that the tighter discipline imposed by

General McNarney was particularly successful.[51] Negative "fraternization" still needed to be eliminated.

Despite this troubling record, there were also positive trends. One of the most intriguing is the demonstrated interest of soldiers in the numerous concerts Germans began to organize after the initial shock of the defeat receded. By the third quarter of 1946, the Army noted that U.S. personnel was attending numerous concerts, art exhibitions, and sporting events with civilians.[52] This more spontaneous mixing was significant just because military authorities did not sponsor it.

It is possible that this interest in German culture was inadvertently stimulated by the Army's efforts to use German artists and performers as cheap entertainment for the GIs. The Heidelberg headquarters *always* had orchestras playing during dinner and supper in all messes.[53] During March 1946 alone, 49 German orchestras performed 869 programs for 321,930 soldiers. 357 civilian variety shows reached 253,600 GIs. Allowing a select group of Germans to sing, play, and dance for their supper may have promoted a growing GI interest in German culture.[54] Perhaps this is why an increasing number of soldiers wished to study the German language.

This other major arena of "positive" fraternization involved German children and had the active support of Army Command. By mid-1946, the Theater headquarters ordered every Army unit to sponsor German Youth Activities (GYA) and then encouraged soldiers and their families to participate as coaches, teachers, and chaperons at the various recreation centers established close to the emerging American military facilities. At first glance, the creation of American-style Boys and Girls Clubs seems apolitically wholesome. General McNarney, however, saw a more significant purpose in American involvement in youth recreation. In his endorsement of what came to be called the GYA, the commanding general wrote:

> It is obvious that one of the most critical problems confronting us is the re-education of the German youth, in order that, as the future leaders of Germany, they will preserve the ideals of Democracy with which we now imbue them . . . the fact that children all over the world "take" to American soldiers

indicates that GI Joe himself is the best demonstrator of Democracy in
action. Many . . . German Youth groups . . . encouraged by the Democratic
spirit displayed by American troops are participating in athletic and cultural
activities. I commend you for the splendid beginning, and encourage you to
continue with this vital program.[55]

Despite McNarney's claim, there is some controversy about the
extent of soldiers' interest in the girls and boys of this newly conquered land. The typical GI's penchant for handing out candy and
gum to begging children may have only indicated a superficial interest in the youth which surrounded him. Nearly all contemporary
accounts agree that the older "frauleins" aroused the interest of
many soldiers more intensely.

Still, even if GI generosity toward children only masked the more
instrumental relations established between soldier and populace, the
gift-giving was real and provided an opportunity for the development of programs that put American troop activities in a much better light. The Christmas season provided the best opportunity for
more organized contacts with German families. Even if the first
occupation pamphlet suggested that the German people were
deserving of contempt, Christmas permitted the temporary suspen-
sion of this official hostility.

The December 1945 Christmas parties were consequently popular with soldiers and children alike. By 1946, however, the Army saw
these events as central to the mission of reconstruction and recon-
ciliation. Consequently, nearly every Army unit sponsored a Christmas event, with an appearance by Santa Claus, and permitted the
distribution of toys to children who were just beginning to experience one of the worst winters in Central European history. The
Adjutant General reported that during this Christmas season, the
Third Army sponsored 1,418 parties, which were attended by
335,315 German children and 28,956 refugee children.

As impressive as these figures are, it is important to keep in mind
that only a relatively small percentage of American troops attended
these parties. Only 7,845 soldiers were on hand at these Christmas
celebrations and a smaller number of dependents (1,577) participated.[56] It is not clear whether or not this latter figure refers to

American children playing with their German contemporaries or wives serving as organizers for these parties.

Other Army documents do suggest that a significant number of Army wives participated significantly in the GYA activities that preceded the Christmas season. American women involved themselves in new programs that could attract German girls. "The most interesting angle of Army relationship [sic] with the civil population can be seen in the increasing importance of the German Youth Activity program, and the number of military and dependent personnel participating has reached high totals. . . . American dependent women have taken a deep interest in German Youth activities in providing instruction and guidance for German girls."[57]

The enthusiasm these activities generated led to the sponsorship of GYA activities by nearly every Third Army unit. By mid-1946, all major commands of the Army had appointed officers to oversee and assist GYA functions. The third quarter report of the Army states: "From 25 July to 31 August, a total of 1730 meetings were held throughout area with 169,497 young people participating in sports events."[58]

Preadolescent German children enthusiastically joined these activities, but adolescents were less forthcoming. Army observers often believed that this "neutral, sometimes hostile" attitude signified greater Nazi contamination.[59] Apparently, such analysts did not consider the possibility that these youth were simply bored older adolescents dismissive of childish activities while hostile to the harsh world of adulthood awaiting them in the aftermath of Germany's cataclysmic defeat. The winning over of the more mature sectors of the German population depended on offering them a more positive future.

Chapter VI

The Beginnings of Gender and Racial Inclusion in the Cold War Military Family

The Decision to Establish Military Communities

The American soldier and his kin paradoxically aided the search for new and more controlled living arrangements for the GI. The demand to reunite families did not only apply to those who wished to return to the United States. A Gallup Poll revealed that a high 64 percent of the American public believed that "wives of servicemen [should] be permitted to visit their husbands who have to stay abroad to police conquered countries." Aside from its potential impact on Germany itself, the decision to permit families to live in Germany (or Japan) lessened two growing problems: the unpopularity of the military because of the continued separation of families and the growing gap in opinion between American men and women over the appropriate conduct for a soldier.

Even the most popular soldier in America was not immune from hostile demonstrations. When the new Chief of Staff, Dwight Eisenhower, visited Capitol Hill in early 1946, for example, he was greeted by soldiers' wives who backed him to the wall. *Life* describes the confrontation in this way: "On his way to Congress to testify on the draft he was hit by a flank attack of wives who wanted their soldiers home. The general beat a strategic retreat into Representative Andrew May's office, but the women broke through and drove him into a corner."[1]

The drive to reunite families was also a response to the tension that emerged within the United States as the public on the home front learned of the reality of fraternization. Only two months after VE Day, the Gallup Poll asked the public whether soldiers "should be allowed to have dates with German girls." Forty-one percent of American men responded yes, while only 22 percent of the women agreed. One woman writing to *Life* wrote the following bitter thanks: "Thank you for telling us what fun it is to 'fraternize'. Too bad there aren't enough Nazi prisoners of war here in America for all of us wives with husbands in Germany to try it."[2]

Given these emerging divisions and the unpromising social relations being established within occupied Germany itself, it is not surprising that the decision to establish military communities came relatively quickly. By the fall of 1945, the Army had already determined its fundamental structure in Germany. First, the Army decided that troops would concentrate themselves in regimental units in particular delimited areas. Second, the Army would allow dependents of at least some, if not all, personnel to enter and remain in occupied areas.[3]

There was some resistance to bringing in wives and children, but the advocates for this move made four key arguments in favor of this move. First, the Army responded to the "flood of anxious letters from the wives of servicemen" by concluding that the importation of American families would improve morale. Second, there was the pious hope that the presence of American families would present to "peoples of the occupied countries good examples of democratic American family and home life." Third, the Command anticipated that the "problems involved in fraternization" would be alleviated. Finally, it was believed that the presence of families would reduce "the number of specially trained men seeking redeployment" back to the States.[4]

On September 19, 1945, the European Theater established a Special Occupational Planning Board responsible to the Chief of Staff. At first, the Board expected that the occupying troops would number around 300,000 and that 90,000 wives and children—both characterized as dependents in Army parlance—would relocate to Germany. Fortunately for the planners, the anticipated size of the Army was cut to about one-third of this figure during 1946.[5]

The planning for this new American invasion relied on the senior officers' experience with the military base or post life of prewar America. The decision to break down American troops into spatially separated regimental units was partially made to replicate the size of military posts in the United States. It was decided to make maximum use of German military facilities, but the conditions would be in keeping with American practices.[6] There was also an effort to make it easier for American families to travel throughout Germany. The Planning Board decided that soldiers with families could buy surplus American vehicles.[7]

The budgetary costs of this policy for the American taxpayer were planned to be limited. The fledgling German governments were supposed to cover the initial construction expenditures as a reparations payment. Moreover, these local governments had to supply and pay for at least one servant for each household—a perk certainly not available to military families in the Zone of the Interior. Those of higher rank (officers and enlisted men of the first three grades) who were just entering Germany were allowed to bring their families with them. Soldiers of any rank already in Germany who agreed to stay one additional year could normally obtain the right to import their families.[8]

The Initial Military Communities

Despite the Army's plans, the initial military communities of the 1940s bore little resemblance to the Army posts in the continental United States. Troops and their mess and recreational facilities were often located in former German Army Kasernen on the outskirts of towns. On the other hand, officers, more often than not, lived in houses and hotels and either received their food within their residences or attended mess set up in hotels or even churches. The arriving American families joined the officers. They resided in requisitioned housing within villages and towns. In some cases, it was possible to create a geographically contiguous territory that could become an enclosed American base. (Frankfurt and Munich had completely fenced-off American territories.) The shrinking of the Army, however, soon changed the attempt to create privileged

American zones within most urban areas. Occupation authorities responded to local German pressure by returning requisitioned houses, and by the late forties "the American community had merged into the German community to such an extent that it was barely to be distinguished except for the signs on the official installation buildings."[9]

It was only later that large-scale construction projects created a base system which was physically isolated from the German population.

The last half of 1946 and early 1947 saw the rapid arrival of American wives and children. By October 12, 1946, 3,780 had relocated in 24 distinct communities.

This influx was only the beginning. By late January 1947, the number of dependents had more than doubled. By the end of the forties, about 30,000 American wives and children resided in Germany.

Logistical Problems

The Army in Germany was not always comfortable with its obligation to facilitate the relocation of American families. The Third Army "Historical Report" one year after VE Day looked back somewhat nostalgically on the glory years of combat:

> It might be well to glance for a moment at the overall picture, and note how entirely different the picture is today in comparison with the days of combat, the contrast being clearly delineated by the needs of yesterday compared with those of today. Then the emphasis was placed on ammunition, clothing and food for fighting men, while today such interesting items as cleaning materials for household use, clothing and feeding of our civilian employees who are natives of the occupied countries and the problem of fresh milk for dependents' children occupy our attention.[10]

The Army historians of the time may have understandably found these housekeeping difficulties trivial in comparison with the combat concerns of the recent past. Nevertheless, those responsible for obtaining households for the incoming Americans were not san-

**Table 6.1   Numbers of Dependents in Military Communities
October 12, 1946**

	0–6	6–14	Ages 14–21	>21	Total
Bamberg	67	40	24	146	277
Kassel	41	22	10	91	164
Nurnberg	75	49	30	256	410
Heidelberg	165	103	38	381	687
Murnau	17	2	0	31	50
Munich	90	62	43	181	376
Augsburg	33	16	3	101	153
Kaufbeuren	2	7	2	15	26
Grafenwohr	19	9	3	42	73
Southofen	20	8	3	36	67
Goppingen	6	3	5	18	32
Bad Tolz	16	5	6	68	95
Amberg	24	27	9	61	121
Berchtesgaden	0	0	0	3	3
Lanshut	8	7	5	33	53
Wetzlar	13	5	2	29	49
Darmstadt	33	17	14	102	166
Stuttgart	107	40	19	233	399
Kitzingen	20	6	4	58	88
Fulda	25	13	9	54	101
Garmisch	4	3	3	18	28
Werden	9	4	2	17	32
Bayreuth	20	14	4	51	89
Regensburg	50	36	11	144	241
Total	864	498	249	2,169	3,780

Sources: Various Monthly Reports, Third U.S. Army, Headquarters, G–1 Section, (Suitland, Md.: National Archives, Record Group 338, Box 67).

guine. Army officials claimed in an April 10, 1946 report: "The USFET system of purchasing household goods from German families on such a large scale would cause great unrest and would be a security threat to our occupation."[11]

Table 6.2   Number of Dependents in Germany

		Ages			
	0–6	*6–14*	*14–21*	*>21*	*total*
12 Oct. 46	864	498	249	2,169	3,780
16 Nov. 46	1,009	560	284	4,123	7,224
25 Jan. 47	2,093	1,081	575	4,679	8,446

Source: Ibid., see Table 6.1.

This comment from the highest levels of the Army in Germany may have stemmed from this March 30 public safety report from the Bavarian occupation government: "The Public Safety Officer, RB Mainfranken, reported ill feeling among the German citizens of Bad Missingen concerning the requisitioning of houses for dependents of troops stationed there. A military policeman guarding the homes was fired upon by an unknown person during the week."[12]

Fear of further overcrowding was one of the main reasons for citizens' unrest. Even before the anticipated inflow of dependents, for example, the city of Heidelberg was housing 25,000 more inhabitants than had lived in the ancient town's environs before World War II. Army Command anticipated the arrival of 25,000 more refugees from the East, as well as a considerable number of women and children from the U.S. The result, the Army feared, could be explosive. "The resulting overcrowded living conditions . . . the rate is already in excess of 2.5 persons for each room . . . coupled with poor sanitation and health standards, may very easily result in a situation presenting definite hazards to troops and dependents."[13]

The Army's own policies also inflamed German opinion. The practice of giving German civilians as little as two hours notice before a property could be seized was a source of constant German complaint. In addition, the Army's Military Government Liaison and Security Offices also asserted that Third Army units tended to hoard property, even though the number of troops in the field was declining rapidly during the first year after VE Day.

This problem existed up until the end of the Third Army's stay in Germany. Its "Report of Operations for the Close-Out Period" notes:

> From time to time throughout the period it was noted that unit and community commanders had been violating existing regulations pertaining to the procurement of real estate. Some of the irregularities noted were:
>
> a. Failure to obtain the concurrence of Military Government before requisitioning German property.
>
> b. Moving units, particularly small detachments, from one area to another without proper authority.
>
> c. Failure to submit an inventory of property within the requisition.
>
> d. Failure of units to submit inventories and requests for real estate on barracks and kasernen.
>
> e. Removing the occupants and occupying property before requisitions have been made and approved by either Military Government or military approving authority.
>
> f. Failure to make out Vacating Forms upon vacating the property.
>
> g. Requisitioning more houses or property than is actually to be used.
>
> h. Failure of Military Community Commanders to plan a housing program in advance in order that Military Government and Town Majors could accomplish necessary work.[14]

For this reason, the Third Army command determined in late 1946 that only the community commanders would have the authority to "obtain sufficient accommodation for all United States and Allied personnel." This general order required the reallocation of single officer and married officer billets, the movement of nonessential troops to less crowded locations, and the rehabilitation of houses already requisitioned, rather than seizing new ones.

These directives could not have been easy to fulfill. The Army began surveys in February 1946 to decide where to place the military community installations for the dependents who would begin to arrive only two months later. It was necessary to hold many coordinating conferences with the G–3, G–4, and engineering unit staffs of the various Army units in order to respond to the many logistical nightmares which this crash program engendered. By March 10, special housing project depots began to receive approximately 25 cars of material per day in Munich, Regensburg, Kassel, and Stuttgart.[15]

The community commanders' requisitioning activities were not supposed to lower German standards of living, but this attempt to limit further acquisitions of property was undercut in two ways. The Army subjected rehabilitation expenses to strict budgetary controls, and no community commander could refuse to accept dependents without the approval of higher authorities. "Prior to disapproving any applications for dependents due to lack of accommodations, community commanders will insure [sic] that all available accommodations under their control have been procured."[16]

The drive to acquire facilities for dependents did not just concern housing. Even more severe was the lack of furniture and consumer durables, which were expected to be part of a modest American household. By June 10, 1946, the Army attempted to put "local furniture factories . . . in operation to assist in the furnishing of quarters for the Heidelberg Area Command."[17] Mobilizing German production for American needs was not a viable solution, since German industry remained far below prewar levels of output. This led the Army to launch an intensive scavenging campaign that undercut its efforts to limit requisitioning. "Authority has been granted major commands to requisition furniture belonging to German civilians which is currently not being used and which is stored in warehouses."[18]

The major reason for this contradictory policies was the inability of the War Department to provide funds for the procurement of construction materials.[19] Once again, financial constraints frustrated the development of a consistent policy. Local officers on the scene were in a quite unenviable position. By early 1947, the procurement crisis loomed large. The following table indicates the huge gap which existed between the items required for the dependents who had arrived in Germany, and the materials actually allocated.

The lack of supplies and housing led to ineffectual protests. As late as January 18, 1947, the Third Army endorsed the recommendation of its commanders in Munich that "Consideration be given to suspending [the] shipment of all dependent families to this theater until such time as additional sources of supply of furnishings

Table 6.3   Deficiencies of Goods for American Dependents

Item	Required	Allocated	% Fulfilled
Refrigerators, Electric	5,454	313	5.7
Ranges, Electric	3,713	851	22.9
Wardrobes	19,788	1,114	5.6
Silverware (Set for 8)	4,736	916	19.3
Chinaware (Set for 8)	3,785	885	22.4
Springs, single	15,601	1,562	10.0
Mattress, single	15,940	1,799	11.3
Pillows	19,496	1,326	6.8

Source: Third U.S. Army, Headquarters, "Report of Operations for the Close-out Period, 1 January–15 February 1947" (Suitland, Md.: National Archives, Record Group 338, Box 80): 56.

and engineer supplies required for dependents are made available."[20] There is no evidence that this request had much impact on the flow of dependents, even though the horrific winter of 1946–47 placed great strain on all of Germany. The pressure to restructure the community life of the American soldier and his family was so intense that the Army was simply forced to cope with the shortages as best it could.

Community Life

Reports on life in Germany from the reunited families suggest that the Army was successful, despite the problems outlined in the previous section. (It is likely that much of the burden of American domestication was placed on the German population.) There was obviously much scrambling for supplies behind the scenes. Moreover, the first families who arrived found themselves without their luggage because dependents' belongings were inexplicably transported on different boats.[21] Nevertheless, as early as the second quarter of 1946, Third Army headquarters reported proudly: "The first contingent of American dependents to arrive in Heidelberg reported that the Red Cross and other agencies combined to make the trip from Bremerhaven a most pleasant one. Meals were said to be excellent, service superior, and the consensus of opinion among the travelers was that the treatment was better than expected."[22]

Once ensconced in their dwellings, the Army wives found themselves faced with surprisingly little trouble. As an early *Life* magazine article notes:"Each happily reunited family settled down comfortably in an undamaged house which was staffed with at least one German servant provided by the Army. . . . The chief worry of the wives was whether to allow their children to play with German children." This concern apparently did not apply to the German women who served as servants and nannies. A photo caption of this *Life* magazine article reads: "In a Berlin Garden a German housekeeper takes care of the children while Mrs. Patrick writes her first letter home."[23]

By early 1947, reports suggest that living standards were quite luxurious. A February 1947 *Life* cover story on the U.S. occupation in Germany focuses on Mrs. Leo Hinkey, wife of a Lieutenant stationed at Furstenfeldbruck Air Forces Replacement Center. The Hinkeys lived in a house originally built for a German officer. The family paid the normal $75 per month rent for their quarters, but spent approximately 40 percent less on food and other supplies than they would have in the United States. In addition, the servant was provided free.[24] *Life* reports that many of the soldiers never had it so good. This is not an exaggeration, if we remember that all of these young adults could vividly remember the struggles of the Depression and the consumption restrictions of wartime.

According to this photo essay, Mrs. Hinkey's daily routine does not appear to have been very stimulating. The typical day, which *Life* describes, began with breakfast of eggs, fresh oranges, and milk. After Lieutenant Hinkey strolled off to work, Mrs. Hinkey gave instructions to her maid and went shopping at the local PX. *Life* describes this stopover as the high point of the morning. The 25–year-old wife was able to sip Cokes, chat with other servicemen and wives, and examine German cameras and watches. Lieutenant Hinkey returned home for lunch, greeted enthusiastically by their (requisitioned?) German shepherd Rolf. According to *Life,* the main privation in Mrs. Hinkey's life was the balky iron stove and the related lack of central heating.[25]

The other institution of family life that the Army had to create from scratch was a system of schools for the children in Germany. This process went surprisingly fast. By October 1946, the schools were already functioning. Kindergarten was not established unless there were at least ten children of the appropriate age. Nevertheless, Armed Forces schools became a central part of military community life. As Army families slowly became transferred to more isolated housing units, mothers and fathers no longer had to worry about American and German children commingling.

The Reconstitution of Gender Relations[26]

The importation of American families rather quickly led to new popular representations of German women. Increasingly, stories appeared in *Stars and Stripes* which portrayed bumbling female servants as dumpy *Hausfrauen* rather than exotic Central European sirens. One cartoon reprinted in *Life* shows a bewildered soldier talking to such a weeping servant while his angry, stylish wife fumes in the background. The caption reads: "But she's my wife, meine Frau, from America. Cantcha Understand?"[27] Perhaps the cartoon tells us why a common bit of advice given to soldiers preparing for their families was to acquire a maid who was not "too good-looking—we don't want any tales out of school."[28]

The change in the marriage policy had a different symbolic effect. The marriage ban had made it more likely that GIs were only interested in German women for sex or laundering. Now, commentators such as Bud Hutton and Andy Rooney argued that more elevated relations could commence. "German young women of virtue and breeding would not . . . associate with Americans . . . because the Army's ban [on marriages] made it all too likely that the soldier's object in such association wasn't matrimony. Legally, it couldn't be."[29] The end of the marriage ban in late 1946 combined with the increasing presence of American women in more isolated American communities to level the sexual playing field. The traditional ease of acquiring American citizenship allowed a limited number of German women to become part of the new family army.[30]

Many commentators have suggested that the arrival of the American woman in Germany and the Americanization of a few German women tamed the American soldier. General Lucius Clay himself stated that: "[Bringing the dependents] gave a stability to our Occupation that I don't think we could have gotten any other way. It brought back a much higher moral standard. I think this was necessary and important."[31]

The actual effects were less dramatic than Clay suggests. There were still many young, unmarried soldiers seeking out German women, who were often willing to engage in sex. As long as Germany remained poor—and economic circumstances did not begin to improve noticeably for the German population until 1948—the field was free for many sexual conquests and conflicts.[32]

The final stabilization of German–American relations depended on the reassertion of German male authority. This, in turn, required the further removal of the American military from German society. The domestication of the American Army in Germany helped the American Army in two ways: Sexual contact between Germans gradually became less frequent and more politically acceptable, and German male elites began to acquire more political and social power within Germany. Slowly, national identity became less important in regulating the power of men over women in early postwar Germany.[33]

The initial sexual contacts between German women and the American soldier threatened to undercut the emerging American commitment to integrate Germany into a Western alliance. The solution reached through a series of adhoc measures was to domesticate the American soldier in Germany by encouraging the presence of American women and children in separate "Little Americas" dotted throughout the West German landscape. In addition, the relatively few native women who formed intense romantic attachments with the young foreign soldiers were eventually permitted to become American through marriage. These policy shifts, along with Germany's political and economic recovery, both transformed the postwar American military and solidified the Western alliance system.

Army Command Resistance to Integration

At the same time Army Command in Germany was taking steps to integrate white women into the military family, resistance continued to the inclusion of black soldiers and their families. The drive to reduce significantly the number of black troops in Europe was temporarily successful. A reader of the primary documents of the Third Army can almost hear the sighs of relief from the headquarters staff as the presence of black troops began to decline in late 1946. In the minds of Army Command and most of their military superiors in the Pentagon, the efforts to weed out blacks helped guarantee a more effective military. "They believed that a ceiling must be imposed on the Army's black strength if a rapid and uncontrolled increase in the number of black troops was to be avoided. And it had to be avoided, they believed, lest it create a disproportionately large pool of black career soldiers with low aptitudes that would weaken the Army."[34] The Army's ill-thought-out emphasis on military efficiency prevailed once again, and by the middle of 1947, the African American presence had dropped in nearly all Army Commands.

The decline in the black presence within the military corresponded with a formal loosening of segregationist practices in the Army, but in a way that the cautious General Marshall would have approved. General Gillem's recommendations included reducing the size of all-black units and making more African American officers commanders of black battalions. In addition, the Gillem report called for the better use of those black soldiers qualified for skilled occupations. This apparent greater openness of the postwar Army, however, could not overcome the firm segregationist opposition within the military, which had lobbied for the reduction in African American forces in the first place.

The sabotage of the Gillem recommendations was not to last.

**Table 6.4[35]   Proportion of African Americans in the U.S. Army
31 December 1946 through 30 June 1947**

	31 December 1946	*30 June 1947*
All Overseas Commands	10.77%	8.75%
European Theater	10.33%	9.95%
Mediterranean Theater	10.05%	8.03%
Alaska	26.6%	14.54%

The continuing difficulties of managing black units remained a concern of Army commanders and their political overseers. Advocates of cautious integration like Marcus Ray continued to press for reform, and the rebellious (or at least challenging) behavior of the African American troops themselves continued to suggest the need for a significant change in Army policies. In other words, the same factors that inspired the Gillem report, in early 1946, were still present in early 1947. Blacks still wished to enter the Army in disproportionately large numbers; some Pentagon officials continued to worry about the costs of segregation; and black opinion continued to call aggressively for the integration of the military. In addition, those who wished to continue segregation had to face a new president who was more aggressively committed to some African American civil rights than Franklin Roosevelt had been.

These factors meant that the Army's racial policies could not be ignored. Already in November 1946, the weekly staff conference noted that the Pentagon had launched "a new study of the long-range plans on the colored situation."[36] By late July 1948, these pressures had culminated in President Truman's Executive Order 9981, which ordered the equal treatment of blacks in the Army. This decision did not necessarily imply that the Administration was ordering racial integration,[37] and the largely segregationist Army Command attempted to exploit the executive order's ambiguous emphasis on equal treatment to maintain that the establishment of separate but equal facilities for black and white soldiers was possible and desirable. The Secretary of the Army, Kenneth Royal, and the new Army Chief of Staff, war hero General Omar Bradley, argued strongly for the continuation of Army racial practices. Bradley was especially worried that "The Army would risk losing its legitimacy with the American public if it moved too fast toward formal racial integration. He [General Bradley] believed that this loss of legitimacy would be manifested in declining enlistment rates—particularly among white southerners."[38]

Significantly, Bradley also argued that the Army could not be held to the same standards as civilian institutions. He stated that desegregating the Army could not be "as simple as integration in public gatherings or places of work during the day."[39] Of course, the opposite proved to be the case. The ultimately successful civil rights campaign to integrate public places in America required the protests of hundreds of thousands, the imprisonment of thousands, and the martyrdom of too many. In contrast, the military was able to use its authoritarian power to require the integration of its public places and operations a decade earlier.

Historians generally agree that the combat requirements of the Korean War, combined with the Truman Administration's pressure, were chiefly responsible for overcoming the Army's staunch opposition to integration. This interpretation is largely correct. However, it would be a mistake to ignore the experience of the occupation in Germany. The success of the quiet efforts of the new military leadership in Germany, starting more than a year before President Truman's 1948 executive order, had already suggested that it would not be overwhelmingly difficult to create a more accommodating set of institutions for black soldiers. The success of those measures that partially included blacks in the training routines of the occupation Army gives us a better understanding of the Army's eventual ability to integrate its black and white soldiers without the enormous disruption that the Army leadership had feared.

When the Third Army was formally disbanded in early January 1947, two committed advocates of racial exclusion, Generals Ernest Harmon and Geoffrey Keyes, also departed. The new commander of European forces was General Lucius Clay—who had previously been second-in-command of the Army in Germany, while taking charge of occupation governance from his office in Berlin. Clay now both continued this task and oversaw the new Army's actions.

Clay's previous record on racial integration was not encouraging. Chapter III documented Clay's opposition to the integration of the occupation government. Still, he did endorse the rigorous training of all his troops in Europe, and he was well aware that a major headache for military government officers had been controlling American troops. The winter of 1946–47 had been exceedingly difficult. German malnutrition was growing, and public dissatisfaction with Germany's continued economic stagnation and political subordination was becoming more noticeable. Clay did not want to worry excessively about his own troops.

To handle the training and direction of the occupation Army, Clay was fortunate to have as his second-in-command General Clarence Huebner, who saw his main task as training and supervising the soldiers who were now settling down in military communities. Huebner had spent most of his military career improving the Army's training policies, and he was probably better suited to facing the challenges of the postwar Army in Europe than a commander who had led combat troops.

Even more significant than Huebner's background was the decision to place Marcus Ray as his advisor. Ray resigned his civilian post at the Pentagon and was commissioned as a Lieutenant Colonel. He decided to use his opportunity in Germany to put into practice some of the policies he had advocated while in the Pentagon. The result was "The most ambitious project by far for improving the status of black troops, and before it was over thousands of black soldiers had been examined, counseled, and trained."[40]

Grafenwoehr in Bavaria was the first sight for this new experiment, because many of the black units that had been in the Third Army resided in this part of Bavaria. Indeed, a relatively segregated military community was being established in this area as a result of this African American concentration. Huebner and Ray decided in March 1947—the same month Clay took over command of the European forces—to implement a 12 to 13 week training program for two black infantry battalions as a pilot project. Morris MacGregor describes the program as follows: "Essentially, he [Huebner] was trying to combine both drill and constant supervision with a broad-based educational program. Trainees received basic military training for six hours daily and academic instruction up to the twelfth grade level for two hours more."[41]

This combination of drill and instruction worked well, and eventually Huebner decided to establish a new training center at Kitzingen Air Base. The plan was to require every black soldier "to participate in the education program until he passed the general education development test for high school level or until he clearly demonstrated that he could not profit from further instruction."[42]

One result of this program was that the soldiers who participated in it on average raised their aptitude test scores significantly—by an average of more than 20 points. Another result was that by 1950—before units were integrated—the venereal disease rate as well as the "serious incident" rate, for black soldiers declined dramatically. By January 1950, observers could no longer legitimately claim that black units were less disciplined and more unruly than white ones.[43]

This change in the training regimen of black troops indicated that institutional intervention could make a significant difference in the deportment of black troops. Racial differences in behavior were not immutable. Moreover, parallel data also revealed that attitudes toward racial segregation could significantly change if the Army modified its personnel policies.

Throughout much of World War II, white opposition to racial integration was almost overwhelming. A survey in 1943 conducted by the Office of War Information with the National Opinion Research Center "revealed that 90 percent of white civilians and 18 percent of black civilians favored keeping white and black troops separate. An Army study prepared that same year concluded that 88 percent of white soldiers and 38 percent of black soldiers believed that blacks and whites should continue to be assigned to separate units."[44]

Apparently, the actual experience of blacks in the Army raised support for segregation among African American soldiers. The reasons most commonly given are that the experiences of black soldiers in the Army led them to believe that they had a better chance for career promotion in their own units and that they would be physically safer if isolated from whites.

By summer 1945, the limited experience with integrated combat in Europe led the Research Branch of the Information and Education Division to interview 250 white officers and noncommissioned officers who had participated in racially mixed infantry companies. "The results revealed that most officers who were familiar with this experiment in race relations had highly positive opinions of it."[45] An additional study of 1,710 white enlisted men confirmed this study. "Among white soldiers who had served in combat units that did not contain black platoons, 62 percent stated that they would greatly dislike serving in a racially mixed unit, and only 18 percent felt that the mixed companies were a good idea. But among whites who had served in divisions that did contain black platoons, just 24 percent indicated aversion to serving in a racially mixed unit, and 50 percent approved of the mixed companies. Only 7 percent of the whites who had actually served in the mixed companies expressed dislike, and 64 percent of these whites held that such units were a good idea."[46]

An interesting footnote to this study is the controversy it generated among the highest levels of the Army. Those who commissioned the study wanted to publish these results, but General Berhon B. Somervell, the commander of Army Service Forces, and General Bradley, at the Headquarters of the European Theater of Operations, persuaded Chief of Staff Marshall that it would be better to shelve these findings. When General Bradley later argued so vociferously for the maintenance of segregation on the grounds that the liberal experimentation would be too disruptive, he knew of compelling evidence to the contrary.[47] The only conclusion a dispassionate observer can draw is that this otherwise quite attractive military commander suffered from a severe racist disorder that prevented him processing information that might challenge his beliefs.

By the late 1940s, a larger white minority expressed itself in favor of racial integration. Now, 63 percent of American adults favored segregation, as opposed to the earlier figure of 90 percent. White soldiers had also moderated their views. In response to a May 1949 survey: "32 percent of the soldiers who responded were 'definitely opposed' to desegregation of any kind, but a slightly higher proportion—39 percent—said that they were 'not definitely opposed.' 61 percent said they were 'definitely opposed to *complete* integration,' but 68 percent expressed tolerance for *partial* desegregation in which blacks and whites worked together but did not share the same barracks or mess halls."[48]

Sherie Mershon and Steven Schlossman argue that these results suggest that many whites opposed integration because they abhorred "close physical or social contact with blacks."[49] Read another way, however, these results imply that once the Army forced contact between blacks and whites, many soldiers realized that their earlier fears were misplaced and irrational and that it was possible to work together productively without any diminution in military efficiency. Some ordinary soldiers realized this before their military superiors did.

Huebner's and Ray's experiments, ironically, took advantage of the realities of segregation in the early postwar Army to create special training facilities for all those black soldiers who required assistance to correct educational deficiencies. The result was that when integration finally came to the Army during the 1950s, the occupation Army in Germany was well placed to implement President Truman's policies. Korean combat requirements may have forced Army Command to search out African Americans as important foot soldiers in the bloody combat. On the other hand, the less dramatic efforts of the occupation Army to make black GIs more effective soldiers made it more likely that the drive to integrate the Armed forces would survive war-fighting exigencies.

By the early 1950s, African American soldiers were finally joining the enlarged military family of the Cold War. The belated inclusion of blacks in the postwar structures of military power is a testament to the strength of segregationist practices and ideology after World War II. It proved to be easier to welcome white women and children than to welcome black men into the occupation army. Nevertheless, the mid-1950s saw the construction of a more unified and inclusive American military than had ever existed before.

Chapter VII

Remaking the Conquering Heroes: Extending American Power

Changing Representations of the GI and German

Even before the January 1946 GI demonstrations, demanding rapid redeployment back to America, many commentators were writing that the U.S. performance in Germany was deeply troubling. Just a few days before the expression of worldwide subaltern anger, a *New York Times* editorial maintained that occupation governance in the American Zone compared unfavorably with that of both the German Soviet Zone and American occupied Japan. "Virtually every newspaper dispatch coming from that zone is a further recital of what must be considered a failure."[1]

The commentaries in the press focused on two major issues: the difficulty of denazification and the problem of inducing appropriate GI behavior. In the former case, it would have been impossible for any military government to satisfy those who quite understandably desired a wholesale purging of German society. On the other hand, limiting misconduct was always one of the major responsibilities of any officer corps—even if the political controversy associated with military misbehavior varied.

Journalistic accounts of GI excesses evolved as the media depiction of the German people shifted. At first, newspapers of record such as the *New York Times* and popular magazines such as *Life* painted an unsympathetic portrait. Most American reporters were hostile to the German people in general, stressing the necessity for ordinary soldiers and citizens to acknowledge their "collective guilt." Later, however, the same press focused on the despair and victimization that the war brought to the innocent German untainted by Nazi association. For example, a *Life* cover photo of three frowning German men on VE Day carries the caption: "The faces of these three German civilians show they know at first hand the bitterness of defeat. . . . Their faces are unhappy but hard and arrogant. Not yet had these Germans . . . been forced to see the atrocities . . . committed in their name."[2] Exactly eight months later, *Life* published a picture of a young German mother mourning over her dead child by the side of a railroad track with a much less political interpretation: "Death March from Lodz in Poland ended in this tragic scene outside Berlin. . . . One three year old boy . . . survived the 270 mile journey, only to die in his mother's arms as she carried him down railroad tracks in Berlin. . . . She lays his body on the tracks while another mother and child weep beside her."[3]

Given this change in the images used to present the German people to an American audience, it is not surprising that the representation of the GI shifted quickly as well. Only six months after VE Day, John Dos Passos, writing in *Life,* reports the following conversation of American officers:

"Don't think I'm sticking up for the Germans," puts in the lanky young captain in the upper berth, "but. . . "

"To hell with the Germans," says the broad-shouldered dark lieutenant. It's what our boys have been doing that worries me."

The lieutenant had been talking about the traffic in Army property, the leaking of gasoline into the black market in France and Belgium even while the fighting was going on, the way the Army kicks the civilians around, the looting.

"Lust, liquor and loot are the soldier's pay," interrupts a red-faced major.

The lieutenant comes out with the conclusion: "Two wrongs don't make a right."

Dos Passos's sympathies are clearly with the lieutenant. He concludes by arguing: "Never has American prestige in Europe been lower. People never tire of telling you the ignorance and rowdyism of American troops."[4]

The low point in American coverage of the GI in Germany came with the October 19, 1946 issue of *Collier's Weekly*. This popular news and literary magazine had already provided critical coverage of the occupation government in Germany. A February 9, 1946 article by Drew Middleton (entitled "Failure in Germany") had, for example, warned: "American Intelligence reports reflect an increasing number of outbursts against American troops during the period when the German soldiers are returning to their homes. The immediate cause is the freedom with which the German women and girls have given themselves to their conquerors."[5] Still, these sorts of stories were interspersed with others celebrating the attempts by American jurists to reintroduce the rule of law in the occupied territory or congratulating the American Army for its efforts to re-educate German POWs who were interned in the United States. The October 19 article by Edward P. Morgan repeated Dos Passos's suggestion that it was American behavior rather than some default in the German character that was responsible for making a difficult situation even worse.

Entitled "Heels among the Heroes," the essay begins with a description of an 18–year-old buck private who "swaggered over" toward a group of impoverished German youths collecting cigarette butts and chased them away. Morgan writes: "The Germans backed off the curb, slowly. The soldier's laughter was brimming with bravado and the heady sweetness of new authority, as he joined a couple of buddies. 'Where did you say that Fraulein lived?' he asked. The enemy stood silent as the trio rounded the corner, but if their smoldering stares had been radioactive, the private would have dropped in his tracks."[6]

Most of the themes documented in the earlier sections of this book are mentioned in Morgan's article. The "Veronika Dankeshoens" are described as "the most tragic lot of all" previous camp followers—presumably because the "Victory Girls" of the training camps in the United States or the "Piccadilly Commandos" of London were on the side of the eventual victors, had more economic options, and were less infected with venereal disease than their German counterparts. The essay, however, does not limit itself—as many of the previous journalistic exposés did—to a discussion of the sexual playing field in Germany. Morgan's article stresses even more heavily the criminal behavior of many of the GIs. As Morgan writes:

> Another of the Army's worries is the frequency of soldier assaults on German civilians. In Bavaria in July, according to official figures, there were 431 incidents involving U.S. troops and Germans. Much of this is blamed on rookie replacements, who never heard a shot fired in anger but are "out to get their Nazis" and thereby establish that they have hair, if not combat medals on their chests.
>
> One evening, a GI stopped a civilian on a lonely street in southern Germany. "Got the time, Mac?" he demanded. The civilian looked at his wrist and answered in English. "Gee mister," the startled soldier said, "It's a good thing you didn't speak Kraut. That's a nice watch you've got there and I'd been thinking I might just take it." The civilian was an Army special agent in plain clothes.[7]

In addition to rampant thievery, the article also documents the legal seizure of property in order to obtain comfortable quarters for the conquering Army. What disturbed Morgan most was the contrast "of that hearty American brightness alongside the gray, squalid existence of urban Germans." The reporter writes:

> You come out of the quartermaster's super commissary in the Onkel Tom subway station in Berlin-Zehlendorf, staggering under a load of fresh Danish whole milk, Kansas steaks, white bread, fresh lemons and butter. You try to cover up this golden swag but a bottle top sticks out brazenly and a lemon spills from the sack and rolls toward the scrawny kids and the hollow-cheeked old woman loitering in the street. You heave the lot into your car, speed home and pour yourself a tall drink, to ponder whether this was an object lesson to prove democracy's triumph over Fascism or a new hate card in the hands of the have-nots.[8]

Morgan's article, like most that get published in popular journals, muddles these descriptions with pious references to the essential decency of the majority of occupation soldiers. He leaves open the possibility that eventually the American presence could bring positive results and help create a new democracy in Germany. Overall, however, the article presents a devastating critique of an inexperienced army of venal adolescents supervised by officers scarcely more mature or moral. Morgan concludes his article with a quote from a soldier's letter in the "B Bag" section of the Army newspaper *Stars and Stripes:*

> I've done things I wouldn't want my parents or sweetheart to see me do, but that's all behind me now. I'll return to those who love me as if nothing had happened. I'll take up my life where I left off, and forget all I did over here. But can I?[9]

Popular Explanations of the GI in Germany

During this time, there were numerous public and private attempts to explain the deplorable behavior of many of the GIs. Edward Morgan, in his *Collier's Weekly* article, placed most of the blame on the chaos of GI redeployment and the importation of adolescent boys who could not cope with either the complex tasks or the temptations they faced in Germany. An officer interviewed for the article explains this perspective when he says: "Here are all the things any self-respecting father would try to keep a high-school boy away from—wine, women and easy side dough to boot—are thrown in the youngster's face. You can't blame the boy. Is he supposed to get religion all of a sudden?[10]

This explanation expands on those narratives discussed in Chapter II that describe the American GI as helpless before the depredations of impoverished, experienced German women. The addition, however, is significant, since many officers acknowledged that the American soldiers were not sweet innocents. Rather, they were unable to resist exploiting their superior power for immoral financial and sexual gain. John Dos Passos captures this theme in a vivid dialogue of soldiers finally returning to America after their tour of duty in Germany:

> "Christ, I've never had so much of it in my life," says a voice out of the dark.
> "I didn't know there was so much of it in the world," answers another.

"You ought to have been in Germany, boy, you just lift your finger and they spread their legs."[11]

Significantly, the title of the book in which this essay appeared is *In the Year of Our Defeat*. Many commentators saw such actions as undermining the U.S. foreign policy goal of constructing a peaceful, stable Europe. Sometimes the sense of betrayal was quite bitter. For example, *Life* correspondent Joe Weston writes: "Before the GIs came most Frenchmen believed the Hollywood version of what Americans are supposed to be but definitely are not . . . They met instead 'democratic' people who hated their own fellow soldiers because they were black. They found 'heart-of-gold sentimentalists' who gave food and candy bars to hungry women but only for a price. They found 'rugged individualists' who treated the local populace as inferior peoples. They found the 'suave, romantic' Americans accosting anything in skirts that walked the streets."[12]

The foreign policy implications of this behavior were quite clear, as noted in *Collier's Weekly*. "American GIs in Germany have a heavy responsibility, yet some of them behave like Peck's Bad Boy. The pay-off will intensify our foreign problems."[13]

Not all of the commentators were as censorious as Dos Passos, Morgan, and Weston. We have already read Julian Bach's defense of American fraternization. Still, even Bach had to place the blame for GI excess somewhere. If the German woman as irresistible siren took some of the blame, then the unnatural, overly aggressive American woman as unnatural taskmaster took the rest. Bach, drawing on the work of the misogynistic Philip Wylie, writes: "If the American man is 'woman-crazy,' it is the American girl who has made him so. That is the funny part about it. In no other culture have women demanded so much attention and respect, tried so hard to make men conscious of their wishes, or entered every phase of their men's lives—business, sport, gambling, drinking—to so great an extent."[14]

Most commentaries of this sort are too simplistic to be any use for serious analysis of the postwar experience. Their only purpose is to highlight the anxieties of that era. Certainly, the constant attempt to "explain" largely male depredations by referring to the corrosive effects of the German and American female character tells us more about postwar male fears than the reality of postwar gender relations.

The temptation to develop half-baked disquisitions on American culture proved irresistible to many commentators. Nor was it difficult, as the last chapter demonstrated, to blame military failings on the alleged inferiority of African American soldiers. Perhaps, the all-too-ready wartime tendency to claim that the German nation could be reduced to Nazi criminality led disillusioned American commentators to apply the same broad brush to explanations of GI immorality. More likely, journalists and other writers attempting to provide quick explanations for disturbing tendencies within the victorious nation found it easier to articulate simple explanations that neglected the more confusing circumstances of postwar reality. To get a deeper understanding of the American soldier and the culture from which he came, we need to look elsewhere.

Gertrude Stein's Critique of American Culture

At first glance, an examination of the truncated postwar commentaries of the American expatriate writer Gertrude Stein seems an unusual place to search for a fuller analysis of the American GI. What would an avant-garde, lesbian writer who had not lived in the United States for decades have to say about the U.S. military? Would not her perceptions of the occupation force be distorted by her own idiosyncratic life?

In fact, Stein, while an expatriate, was always a rather ardent American patriot. It might be said that she was in love with the idea of America, but repulsed by much of its reality. It is this ambiguity that makes her writings on the GI so fascinating. By all accounts, Stein deeply enjoyed her trips to the American troops in Germany and France. One of her biographers notes that from September 1944 until her death, Stein "surrounded herself with young GIs."[15] Perhaps the military encouraged Stein's visits to American soldiers in Germany and France so that they could embrace a higher cultural level than that of the barracks. It is doubtful that Stein had any elevated effect on the soldiers she met, but her journalistic and fictional writings of these encounters leave a fascinating record.

Take Stein's scolding of American GIs in an August 1945 *Life* article: "I got very angry with them, they admitted they liked the Germans better than other Europeans. Of course you do, I said, they flatter you and they obey you, when the other countries don't like you and say so. . . . Well said one of them after all we are on top. Yes I said and is there any spot on earth more dangerous than on top."[16]

Here, Stein places herself at the center of a GI conversation, argues with the soldiers, and suggests that their present superiority betrays weakness and confusion. Stein's willingness to argue also suggests an ability to listen sympathetically to people whose behavior she might otherwise deplore. Stein is also unique because she is willing to challenge military hierarchy. Her *Life* article, for example, celebrates American indiscipline and urges the GI to teach the German population American anarchistic tendencies. It is this amused engagement and subtle attempts to delegitimate the authoritarian aspects of the occupation that sets Stein's commentaries apart from others who write about the immediate postwar era.

Stein's last major work, published three days before her death from stomach cancer, appeared in 1946. *Brewsie and Willie* is "a dialogue in American slang between a group of GIs who think aloud the problems they will face when they return to America. They discuss fraternization, women, American sexual drive, 'lousy foreigners', industrialism in the United States, American blacks, the loss of the 'pioneer spirit' and the increase of a job mentality at home and the impending future decline of America."[17]

This description of the novel does not completely explain Stein's purpose. Unlike other American writers who seemed to shrink back in despair from the rootlessness and alienation that apparently infected the typical American GI, Stein, as a permanent American in exile, found this condition liberating. The absence of family ties and the uncertainty of place gave the largely ignorant youths she depicts in *Brewsie and Willie* a freedom that they had never experienced before. It is as if she was welcoming the soldiers into the dislocations of her own expatriate existence.

The circumstances of the American soldier also recalled for Stein the romantic pioneer or frontier spirit that she believed was the essence of American exceptionalism. Unfortunately, she saw that the tedium and boredom of the present threatened to undermine the future adventures that beckoned. The character Brewsie serves as a gadfly to disturb the judgments of his fellow soldiers. He tries to upset their equilibrium just as the surrounding environment does in order to leave them dissatisfied and questing.

As with most other writers, Stein begins her descriptions of the occupation by considering sex and fraternization. The first few paragraphs read:

> You know, Willie, said Brewsie, I think we are all funny, pretty funny, about this fraternization business, now just listen. They did not have to make any anti-fraternization ruling for the German army in France because although the Germans did their best to fraternize, no French woman would look or speak to them or recognize their existence. I kind of wonder would our women be like French or be like Germans, if the horrible happened and our country was conquered and occupied.

> Willie: Well I wouldnt want any American woman to be like a French-woman.
> Brewsie: No you would want them to be like the Germans, sleep with the conquerors.
> Willie: You get the hell out of here, Brewsie. No American woman would sleep with a foreigner.
> Brewsie: But you admire the Germans who do. Which do you want American women to be like?
> Willie: I know what I dont want them to be like, I dont want them to be like any lousy foreigner.
> Brewsie: But all our fathers and mothers were lousy foreigners.
> Willie: You get the hell out of here, Brewsie. What's that to you, I am going to sleep with any German wench who'll sleep with me and they all will.[18]

Stein's text never resolves these questions. Instead, Brewsie keeps asking Willie and others to listen, and they usually do because they have nothing to do while waiting for redeployment. One of the GIs, Brock, is older than the rest. He likes to talk about his parents because: "He was interested in everything they wrote to him and was natural enough because although he had been married, he did not know whether he was married or not."[19] Brock holds fast to his parents and the shaky domesticity they represent.

> Brock: No no I am not disillusioned, as long as my mother is fond of flowers, and she is and fond of cooking as she is and fond of eating as she is, and likes to move into other houses which she does I could never be that word I could never be disillusioned. No, Jo, no, no no, and I think you all know I mean it I do I never could be disillusioned.
>
> Willie: Take me away, that man makes me crazy. I just cant stand another minute of it, take me away.[20]

Stein paints a picture of GIs who do not want to think dangerous thoughts, but who are repulsed by the simple-minded domesticity which Brock celebrates. It is this tension that *Brewsie and Willie* exploits. The dislocation that idleness brings separates the GI from any particular location. They are, as a group, on their own. "While they were talking they did not know what country they were in. If they did know they might talk about it but they did not know what country they were in, and little by little they knew less what country they were in."[21]

Nor is there any authority the GI can turn to. "It used to be fine, said Willie, before the war when we used to believe what the newspapers and the magazines said, we used to believe them when we read them and now when it's us they write about we know it's lies, just lies, just bunches of lies, and if it's just bunches of lies, what we going to read when we get home, answer me that, Brewsie, answer me that."[22]

Throughout *Brewsie and Willie,* home constantly beckons—even if no one can quite define it. For Brewsie, home means suffocating comfort similar to what exists for the GI in Europe, but with the tedium of financial worry. "Well dont we have food and clothes and shoes and free parties all the time, they take us everywhere, and eats, and treats, and free everything, subways and theatres and everything and my gracious, my good gracious. I just could kind of just cry when I think we all got to scratch around and worry, worry and scratch around, and then those bills, pay everything on the installment plan, and coming in and coming in, oh dear, sometimes I just burst out crying in my sleep, I am older than you boys, you dont know, I could just burst out crying."[23]

Stein's fear of the future revolves around her distaste for industrial capitalism and her desire that every soldier could become a free man.

> Yes but Willie, said Brewsie, that's what I want to say, industrialism which produces more than anybody can buy and makes employees out of free men makes 'em stop thinking, stop feeling, makes 'em feel alike. I tell you Willie it's wrong.
>
> You know, said Willie, what you make industrialism sound like, you make it sound like chewing gum. You chew and chew but it dont feed you, it's got a kind of a taste but that is all there is to it no substance. Have I got it right, kind of? Industrialism is like chewing gum.[24]

Stein's economic prognostications are shaky. (She constantly predicts the return of the Great Depression.) Her presentation of an anti-industrial alternative is utopian and reactionary. (In her attack on big unions, big capitalists, and the welfare state, there is more than a whiff of fascist ideology.) Still, her emphasis on the softness of domesticity and her attempt (through Brewsie) to induce GIs to use their alienated freedom to forge a new America of independent-thinking citizens is compelling.

She wants soldiers to think, and she holds out the hope that Americans will embrace a new patriotism that celebrates an older (and mythological) pioneer spirit that neither yields to economic exigencies nor succumbs to the temptation to dominate others.[25] The confusion, alienation, and cynicism of the occupation period is seen by Stein as an opportunity both to escape the industrial softness which beckons and to eschew being "the strong white man, who can never be brought down."[26] Stein is much less censorious than other commentators on the GIs, but she also unrealistically demands more. She wants them to use their experiences in Europe to escape the bubble gum society of domesticated industrialism and national chauvinism.

The Imperial Frontier of the Mid-Twentieth Century

Gertrude Stein's constant attempt to cajole the GIs back to a frontier sensibility makes use of perhaps the most famous historical framework in American historiography. Near the end of the nineteenth century, Frederick Jackson Turner argued in his essay "The Significance of the Frontier in American History" that the experience of westward settlement largely defined the early history of the United Sates. He saw the frontier as both "a meeting point between savagery and civilization" and "the line of most rapid and effective Americanization."[27]

It is not difficult to challenge Turner's anxious desire (during the age of the Ku Klux Klan and lynching) to deemphasize the importance of race and slavery in American history. Nor is it hard to dispute his views of the "barbaric" indigenous populations of the American continent. On the other hand, Turner's emphasis on the conflicts and challenges that arise from the movement of cultural and political boundaries remains key to the understanding of American historical change. The mid-twentieth century United States faced its own moving boundaries, and there were some similarities between the early American and mid-twentieth century frontiers. The squalor and the easy availability of sexual services made Germany seem like a series of frontier towns of early Western settlement. The presence of roving armed bands occasionally acting with criminal intent also recalls the "wild" aspect of the earlier American frontier experiences.

The provocative similarities between the settling of the West and the soldier settlements in defeated Germany that Stein draws on should, however, not lead us astray. If the first 300 years of European settlement resulted in the creation of a distinctive American character and polity, the twentieth-century construction of the American empire confronted the U.S. political and economic elite with older European dilemmas. Indeed, the attempt to establish lines of control throughout the world bore a close resemblance to what Turner labeled the traditional European frontier—"a fortified boundary line running through dense populations."[28] This is the great irony facing any historian interpreting the just-completed "American century"— the decline of populist American particularity as American political, economic, and cultural institutions spread throughout the world.

Turner emphasizes in his essay the impossibility of controlling the movements of European peoples westward. In the late 1940s, there were no unregulated movements of Americans into Germany. Despite their lack of discipline, the American soldier always remained subject to a powerful corporate authority. Very few soldiers of the occupation wished to remain in Europe. Like the garrison soldier of the past, they longed to return home—not settle in a new frontier. This reality gave military authorities the opportunity to construct protected American enclaves that placed willing GIs under more effective control.

Stein herself was well aware that the possibilities she saw in the squalor of the occupation were being undermined by this military policy. She writes of "all those men all that army going around excursioning in auto-buses, so fat, so well-dressed, so taken care of."[29] Ultimately, it is the return to a real place called home which destroys Stein's hopes. As Willie and other soldiers leave for home, they have a final conversation with the two American women who have joined the GIs' long conversations:

> And tell me, said Janet, wont you miss talking when you get home, you do know dont you all of you nobody talks like you boys were always talking, not back home. Yes we know, said Jo. Yes we know, said Jimmie. Not Brewsie, said Willie, he'll talk but, said Willie, Brewsie will talk but we wont be there to listen, we kind of will remember that he's talking somewhere but we wont be there to listen, there wont be anybody talking where we will be. But, said Jo, perhaps they will talk now, why you all so sure they wont talk over there, perhaps they will talk over there. Not those on the job they wont, said Willie, not those on the job.[30]

The demonstrations in January 1946 signaled to most commentators a disturbing lack of discipline and self-control. Read another way, however, the soldiers' united action more deeply represented the GIs desire to be reintegrated into the "soft," industrial American society that Stein so deeply deplored.

The Conquering Heroes Join The Imperial Military Family

Brewsie and Willie inadvertently suggested that one solution to the GI problem would be to isolate the troops from the "dirty, lousy foreigners" and to care for them with those comforts that only American wealth could provide. Legitimizing the American presence required both providing a comfortable, non-threatening life for the soldiers and their dependents and separating the GI more radically from German society. Given the realities of the racial composition of the Army in Germany, African American soldiers would also have to join this imperial military family.

The success of the domesticating reforms of the late 1940s permitted President Truman to double the troop presence during the Korean War crisis with few complaints from the new German state. The controversy of this measure centered only on geopolitical calculation, not the worry that the U.S. Army would be unable to control the American soldier and thus destabilize Europe. John Dos Passos' moralistic critique of the American presence no longer resonated.

From exceedingly troubling postwar circumstances, the U.S. foreign policy establishment emerged much strengthened in Europe. The military developed policies that permitted the permanent extension of U.S. power in Europe. Americans became used to the idea that the world required their military presence. They became used to the ideas that military engagement would normally require only limited sacrifices, but that all citizens—black and white as well as male and female—would be allowed to be part of military life. Americans became the soft citizens that Gertrude Stein envisioned. Exploring human potential became associated with mass consumption and career advancement. Indeed, military and civilian society became more and more like each other.

This convergence did not proceed smoothly, but Vietnam-era crises ultimately intensified efforts by the Pentagon to "normalize" military employment. The abolition of conscription became linked to the appearance of new public relations campaigns that effectively sold the military as an institution that could provide young adults with skills and attributes necessary for the pursuit of successful professional careers, both inside and outside the military. Without the domesticating successes of the early Cold War Army, it is doubtful that such a marketing strategy would have been so triumphant.

The basic model of military life that the Army developed in the immediate postwar years has now survived the Cold War era. The American military remains a legitimate and popular institution essential to the maintenance and extension of contemporary American power. The swaggering, sometimes anarchistic conquering heroes of World War II no longer exist. Their remaking means that the troubling and promising features of military life during that heroic era have ceased. Internal challenges to American imperial authority will only come from other sectors of the U.S. polity.

Notes

Introduction

1. The other two key locations are Japan and the United Kingdom.
2. Daniel J. Nelson, *A History of U.S. Military Forces in Germany* (Boulder: Westview Press, 1987).
3. In late 1945, President Truman told Secretary of State Byrnes that domestic issues had to take priority over international affairs. Truman's views, not surprisingly, echoed those of public opinion pools, which indicated that the American public did not clamor for a tough interventionist foreign policy. The main desire of Americans seemed to be to get "the boys" home and cut taxes. These views did not change dramatically during early 1946—when the reality of the Cold War began to emerge. Only 7 percent of the American people considered foreign affairs to be of vital importance during the autumn of 1945. The figure was only 11 percent eight months later, in June 1946. See Melvyn P. Leffler, *A Preponderance of Power: National Security, the Truman Administration, and the Cold War* (Stanford, Calif: Stanford University Press, 1992): 46, 52, 97, 106.
4. Lucius Clay, "Proconsul of a People, by Another People, for Both Peoples," *Americans as Proconsuls: United States Military Government in Germany and Japan, 1944–1952.* Robert Wolfe (ed.) (Carbondale: Southern Illinois Press, 1984): 107.
5. Edward N. Peterson, "The Occupation as Perceived by the Public, Scholars, and Policy Makers," in *Americans as Proconsuls:* 424.
6. George Kennan, *Memoirs* (London: Hutchinsons of London, 1968): 372.

Chapter I

1. Joe Weston, "We Wanna Go Home," *Life,* January 21, 1946: 36.
2. "U.S. Prestige Drops after GI Protests: High Officers Say Occupation of Germany is Affected-McNarney Urges Halt," *New York Times,* January 13, 1946: 1.
3. Ibid.
4. Ibid.: 5.
5. The Council of Foreign Relations consistently advocated a soft peace throughout the war. See the series of essays compiled under the title *Studies of American Interests in the War and the Peace* (New York: Council of Foreign Relations, early 1940s). Moreover, those occupation authorities which had been trained in America and Britain before arriving in Germany had studied the Army's own analysis of the World War I occupation experience. The author of the most important Army report, Col. Erwin Hunt, had concluded that the primary mission of an occupation government should be to make friends of former enemies. See Earl F. Ziemke, "The Formulation and Initial Implementation of U.S. Occupation Policy in Germany," in Hans A. Scmitt (ed.), *U.S. Occupation in Europe after World War II: Papers and Reminiscences from the April 23–24, 1976 Conference Held at the George C. Marshall Research Foundation, Lexington, Virginia* (Lawrence: The Regents Press of Kansas, 1978): 42.
6. Earl F. Ziemke, "The Formulation and Initial Implementation of U.S. Occupation Policy in Germany," in Hans A. Scmitt (ed.), *U.S. Occupation in Europe after World War II: Papers and Reminiscences from the April 23–24, 1976 Conference Held at the George C. Marshall Research Foundation, Lexington, Virginia* (Lawrence: The Regents Press of Kansas, 1978): 42.
7. Ibid.: 19–20.
8. Much of the information in this section is taken from Hans-Juergen Schrott, "U.S. Forces in Germany, 1946–1955," in Simon W. Duke and Wolfgang Krieger (eds.) *U.S. Military Forces in Europe, The Early Years, 1945–1970* (Boulder, Colo.: Westview Press, 1993): 153–80.
9. Patton was removed from command of the Third Army in October 1945. He died in an automobile accident in December of that year. Patton's replacement, Lieutenant General Truscott, became ill in early 1946 and was replaced by Keyes, who remained in command until the Third Army was disbanded in early 1947.
10. Hans-Juergen Schrott, "U.S. Forces in Germany, 1946–1955": 160.
11. Oliver J. Frederiksen, *The American Military Occupation of Germany, 1945–1953* (Headquarters, United States Army Europe, Historical Division, 1953).

12. Harold Zink, *American Military Government in Germany* (New York: Macmillan, 1947): 105–109.

13. Edward N. Peterson, "The Occupation as Percveived by the Public, Scholars, and Policy Makers": 420.

14. Winston S. Churchill, *Triumph and Tragedy: The Second World War,* vol. 6 (Boston: Houghton-Mifflin, 1953): 353.

15. Harold Zink, *American Military Government in Germany:* 137–8.

16. Ibid.

17. Ibid.

18. "Report for the Month of October 1945," Provost Marshal's Section, Third U.S. Army (Suitland, Md.: National Archives, Record Group 338, Box 78).

19. Franklin M. Davis, Jr. reports that "By January 1946, there was a marked increase in major crimes involving soldiers. The serious incident rate showing the number of crimes reported in a given month per thousand men, rose from 3.7 in August 1945, to a peak of 11.1 in January 1946." Franklin M. Davis, Jr., *Came as a Conqueror: The United States Occupation of Germany* (New York: Macmillan, 1967): 171.

20. Earl F. Ziemke, *The U.S. Army in the Occupation of Germany, 1944–46* (Washington, D.C.: Center of Military History, United States Army, 1985): 437–8.

21. Various "Historical Reports" in Provost Marshal's section of quarterly "Report of Operations," Third U.S. Army. (Suitland, Md.: National Archives Record Group 338, Boxes 66 and 67).

22. U.S. Army Forces in the U.S. European Theater (USFET), "Occupation" (1946): 9–10.

23. Earl F. Ziemke, *The U.S. Army in the Occupation of Germany, 1944–46:* 336.

24. Julian Bach, Jr., *America's Germany: An Account of the Occupation* (New York: Random House, 1946): 58.

25. The reason for this is that "a perfunctory oath" was sufficient to qualify almost any accumulated earnings as gambling profits. Earl Ziemke states, "Probably no army ever had so many successful gamblers." Earl F. Ziemke, *The U.S. Army in the Occupation of Germany 1944–46:* 336–7.

26. Davis also notes that many benefits were not tradable. "GIs could drink 10 cent martinis in a hotel converted to a service club and take a free special to Berechtesgaden and stay there for not more than $3 a day." Franklin M. Davis, Jr., *Came as a Conqueror:* 138–9.

27. John H. Backer, *Priming the German Economy: American Occupational Policies, 1945–1948* (Durham, N.C: Duke University Press, 1971).

28. Julian Bach, *America's Germany:* 70.

29. Ibid.: 64.

30. Earl F. Ziemke, *The U.S. Army in the Occupation of Germany,* 1944–46: 338.

31. *Hearings Before the Committees on Appropriations, Armed Services and Banking and Currency,* U.S. Senate 80th Congress, First Session on Occupation Currency Transactions (Washington, D.C.: GPO, 1947): 97.

32. Ibid.: 59.

33. "Americans Steal Hessian Jewels," *Life,* June 24, 1946.

34. "GI Gang Seized in Boxcar: Directed Freight Robberies from Swank Rail Hideout in Germany," *New York Times,* January 5, 1946: 7.

35. Oliver J. Frederiksen, *The American Military Occupation of Germany, 1945–53:* 66. According to Frederiksen, the rate of disappearance declined throughout 1946.

36. Ibid.: 70.

37. John Gimbel, *A German Community under Occupation* (Stanford, Calif.: Stanford University Press, 1961): 69–70.

38. Calvin Hoover, *Memoirs of Capitalism, Communism and Nazism* (Durham, N.C.: Duke University Press, 1965): 227.

39. "Shortly after our arrival in Frankfurt, we carried out 'Operation Tally-Ho.' Roadblocks were set up, and houses and persons searched by our troops in order to search for Nazi leaders who might be hiding, our own AWOL's, concealed arms, stolen governmental property, and so on. According to plan, the operation was to cover the entire population. In the process our troops quite generally looted cameras, radios, field glasses, and even personal jewelry." Ibid.: 227.

40. Earl F. Ziemke, *The U.S. Army in the Occupation of Germany, 1944–46:* 397–8.

41. Calvin Hoover, *Memoirs of Capitalism, Communism and Nazism:* 228. One wonders if other phrases of the sixties, such as the use of the word "liberating" for stealing, come from the occupation Army. For the development of requisitioning practices in Italy, see Robert Neville, "Army Requisitions: U.S. Soldiers Appropriated Everything in Sight," *Life,* April 8, 1946. Neville argues that units that had native speakers of Italian were particularly effective in scrambling for property. It would be interesting to know if German speakers in the American Army played a similar role.

42. Robert Murphy, *Diplomat among Warriors* (Garden City: Doubleday, 1964): 293.

43. Lucius Clay, "Proconsuls of a People, by another People, for Both Peoples," in Wolfe, *Americans as Proconsuls:* 107.

44. Oliver J. Frederiksen, *The American Military Occupation of Germany, 1945–1953:* 120.

45. Julian Bach, *America's Germany:* 32.

46. See John Gimbel, *A German Community under American Occupation:* 54–5,

and Edward N. Peterson, *The American Occupation of Germany: Retreat to Victory* (Detroit, Mich.: Wayne State University, 1977): 194–5.

47. John Gimbel, *A German Community under American Occupation*: 84. See also the Chief of Staff section of the Third Army's "Report for the Month of December 1945." This report states, "There is widespread abuse of hunting and fishing privileges. Our present license system is ineffective and the regulations are greatly ignored. All types of weapons are being used. There is much slaughtering of game and leaving of wounded animals in the woods to die. New drastic regulations are being written which must be enforced. There is evidence that ammunition left over from hunting trips is used to shoot at signs, lights, and even at houses." "Report for the Month of December 1945," History of the Command Section, Headquarters, Third Army (Suitland, Md.: National Archives, Record Group 338, Box 66).

Chapter II

1. John Willoughby, "The Sexual Behavior of American GI's during the Early Years of the Occupation of Germany," *Journal of Military History* 62 (January 1998): 155–74.

2. Third U.S. Army Headquarters, "Report of Operations 1 January–31 March 1946" (Suitland, Md.: National Archives, Record Group 338, Box 80): 23.

3. Ibid.: 29.

4. Third U.S. Army Headquarters, "Report of Operations, 1 July–30 September 1946" (Suitland, Md.: National Archives, Record Groups 338, Box 80): 13.

5. Third U.S. Army Headquarters, "Report of Operations, 1 April–30 June 1946" (Suitland, Md.: National Archives, Record Group 338, Box 80): 17.

6. Third U.S. Army Headquarters, "Report of Operations 1 October–31 December 1946" (Suitland, Md.: National Archives, Record Group 338, Box 80): 30.

7. Earl F. Ziemke, *The U.S. Army in the Occupation of Germany, 1944–1946*: 324.

8. Harold Zink, *American Military Government in Germany*: 239.

9. Life reports that after the lifting of the ban on fraternizing with children, GIs would often greet German "girls" with: "Good day child." "German Girls: U.S. Army Boycott Fails to Stop GIs from Fraternizing with Them," *Life*, July 23, 1945: 35.

10. Oliver J. Frederiksen, *The American Military Occupation of Germany, 1944–1953*: 136.

11. Ibid.: 137.

12. John Gimbel, A German Community under American Occupation: Marburg: 69.

13. "Fraternization: The Word Takes on a Brand-New Meaning in Germany," *Life,* July 2, 1945: 26. Julian Bach, Jr., *America's Germany:* 76.

14. Alec Cairncross, *A Country to Play With: Level of Industry Negotiations in Berlin 1945–46* (Gerrards Cross: Colin Smythe, 1987): 45.

15. Julian Bach, Jr., *America's Germany:* 76.

16. David Reynolds, *Rich Relations: The American Occupation of Britain, 1942–1945.* (New York: Random House, 1995): 81.

17. Earl F. Ziemke, *The U.S. Army in the Occupation of Germany, 1944–46:* 327.

18. Oliver J. Frederiksen, *The American Military Occupation of Germany, 1944–1953:* 159.

19. Ibid.: 109.

20. *Life* magazine makes the hunger for sex among combat troops clear in its article on GI conduct in France before VE Day. See John Neill, "*Life* Reports: Vooli Voo, Mamzelle: GIs in Paris Solve Love and Language Problems," *Life,* April 30, 1945. More to the point, Cosmas and Cowdry report: "The VD rate among former combat troops, only a fourth that of [support] forces while the fighting continued, rose rapidly after VE Day, equaling and then surpassing the rate among support troops." Graham A. Cosmas and Albert E. Cowdry, *Medical Service in the European Theater of Operations:* The Medical Department. (Washington, D.C.: Center of Military History, United States Army, 1992): 584.

21. Ibid.: 585. See also Earl F. Ziemke, *The U.S. Army in the Occupation of Germany, 1944–46:* 355.

22. Much of this approach was modeled on the Army's campaign against VD in Britain. Between 1942 and mid-1944, the rate of new cases per 1,000 troops per year declined from 58 to 20. See Graham A. Cosmas and Albert E. Cowdry, *Medical Service in the European Theater of Operations:* 147. For a description of the VD campaign in Britain, see David Reynolds, *Rich Relations:* 201–205.

23. Ibid.: 542.

24. Ibid.: 540.

25. Dr. Arthur G. Volz, selections from Report of Liaison and Security Office, provided by Dr. Volz to author.

26. Ibid.

27. Ibid.

28. Earl F. Ziemke, *The U.S. Army in the Occupation of Germany, 1944–46:* 327.

29. "A USFET letter concerning 'social passes' was indorsed [sic] to Third Army

units directing that physical examinations will not be a requirement for the issuance of a social pass, nor will the files of Health Bureaus be checked." G-1 Section, Third U.S. Army, "Report for the Month of November 1946." (Suitland, Md.: National Archives, Record Group 338, Box 68).

30. Cynthia Enloe, *Bananas, Beaches and Bases: Making Feminist Sense of International Politics.* (Berkeley: University of California Press, 1989): 67.

31. Bud Hutton and Andy Rooney, *Conquerors' Peace: Report to the American Stockholders* (New York, Doubleday and Co., 1947): 36. Hutton and Rooney also report that soldiers enjoyed persecuting young German women by attempting to hook their ankles while driving by in jeeps. Access to motorized vehicles became a symbol of male power in Germany.

32. Julian Bach, Jr., *America's Germany:* 110.

33. Ibid.

34. Quoted in Edward N. Peterson, *The American Occupation of Germany: Retreat to Victory:* 291.

35. Theodore Singer, Letter to the Editor, *New York Times,* Nov. 30, 1945: 12.

36. John Gimbel, *A German Community under Occupation:* 69–70.

37. "*Life* Visits a German University," *Life,* August 19, 1946, 110.

38. Walter J. Slatoff, "GI Morals in Germany," *The Nation,* May 13, 1946: 686–7. Mr. Slatoff edited the 310th Regiment's newspaper "The Lightning Bug" for two years and served in Europe for a year and a half.

39. Ibid.

40. "Fraternization: The Word Takes on a Brand-New Meaning in Germany," *Life,* July 2, 1945: 26.

41. "Women in Heidelberg used bazookas, grenades against the Americans. Others left poisoned candy behind in their homes to entice Allied soldiers or put grenades inside disemboweled rats to make booby traps." "The Nazi State Dissolves," *Life,* April 9, 1945: 46.

42. Tania Long, "The Longing for a New Fuehrer: German Women are Bitter, Hostile and Fearful of the Future; Yet They Are Still Steeped in Nazi Poison," *New York Times Sunday Magazine,* December 9, 1945. Long did not just make this story up. She refers to an Army survey in Darmstadt that claimed that 68 percent of the surveyed women had Nazi sympathies compared to 38 percent of men. Evidently, the survey indicated that women were more likely to complain about the American occupation and were more likely to endorse statements suggesting that Germany needed an authoritarian leader to solve its problems.

43. Julian Bach, Jr., *America's Germany:* 76. See also "German Girls: U.S. Army Boycott Fails to Stop GIs from Fraternizing with Them," *Life,* July 23, 1945: 35.

44. Harold Zink, *American Military Government in Germany:* 239.

45. "Life Spends a Day with a GI Occupying Germany," *Life,* February 10, 1947: 144.

46. Franklin M. Davis, Jr., *Came as a Conqueror:* 144.

47. Julian Bach, Jr., *America's Germany:* 32.

Chapter III

1. Mary Penich Motlet (ed.), *The Invisible Soldier:* The Experience of the Black Soldier (Detroit, Mich.: Wayne State University, 1975): 13.

 2. Morris J. MacGregor, Jr., *Integration of the Armed Forces 1940–1945* (Washington, D.C.: Center of Military History, 1981): 131. See also Mershon and Schlossman, who argue that white military officers articulated two rationales for segregation—the "sociological" and "ontological." The evidence suggests that General Marshall was a firm believer in the "separate but equal" doctrine that provided constitutional cover for racial discrimination. To his credit, however, Marshall did occasionally complain about the unequal justice and unequal facilities that blacks in the Army received. Sherie Mershon and Steven Schlossman, *Foxholes and Color Lines: Desegregating the U.S. Armed Forces* (Baltimore, Md.: The Johns Hopkins University Press, 1998): 13–24 and 92.

 3. Gary A. Donaldson, *The History of African-Americans in the Military* (Malabar, Fla.: Krieger Publishing Co., 1991): 105–111.

 4. Phillip McGuire, *Taps for a Jim Crow Army* (Santa Barbara, Calif.: ABC-Clio, 1983): xxiv.

 5. Sherie Mershon and Steven Schlossman, *Foxholes and Color Lines:* 103.

 6. Neil A. Wynn, The Afro-American and the Second World War (New York: Holmes and Meier, 1993): 31. See also Sherie Mershon and Steven Schlossman, *Foxholes and Color Lines:* 54.

 7. Sherie Mershon and Steven Schlossman, *Foxholes and Color Lines:* 57.

 8. Ibid.: 124–5.

 9. Ibid.: 59 and 73. White soldier support for segregation was quite high. A 1943 survey revealed that 88 percent of whites in the Army wanted segregation maintained.

10. Morris J. MacGregor, Jr., *Integration of the Armed Forces:* 131.

11. Ibid.: 151.

12. Ibid.: 139.

13. Ibid.: 143.

14. Sherie Mershon and Steven Schlossman, *Foxholes and Color Lines:* 117.

15. Bernard Nalty and Morris J. MacGregor, Jr., (eds.), *Blacks in the Military:*

Essential Documents. (Wilmington, Del.: Scholarly Resources, Inc., 1981): 211.

16. Ibid.: 217.

17. Sherie Mershon and Steven Schlossman, *Foxholes and Color Lines:* 96.

18. Morris J. MacGregor, Jr., *Integration of the Armed Forces:* 152.

19. Ibid.: 179.

20. Ibid: 130.

21. Bernard Nalty and Morris J. MacGregor, Jr. (eds.). *Blacks in the Military: Essential Documents:* 212.

22. Morris J. MacGregor, Jr., *Integration of the Armed Forces:* 211.

23. White soldiers who had participated with blacks in combat exhibited significantly more liberal racial views. Sherie Mershon and Steven Schlossman, *Foxholes and Color Lines:* 141–2.

24. Mary Penich Motley (ed.), *The Invisible Soldier:* 191.

25. Ibid.: 191.

26. Ibid.

27. Bernard Nalty and Morris J. MacGregor, Jr. (eds.) *Blacks in the Military: Essential Documents:* 217.

28. A similar phenomenon was also observed in Hawaii. Most populations seem to have discriminatory attitudes and practices, but it does not follow that such discrimination is automatically transferred to an outside group. Sherie Mershon and Steven Schlossman, *Foxholes and Color Lines:* 85.

29. Morris J. MacGregor, Jr., *Integration of the Armed Forces:* 210.

30. Ibid.: 214–215.

31. Bernard Nalty and Morris J. MacGregor, Jr., (eds.), *Blacks in the Military: Essential Documents:* 211.

32. Third U.S. Army Headquarters, Chief of Staff Section, "Report of Operations, 1 January–31 March 1946" (Suitland, Md.: National Archives, Record Group 338: Box 80): 11. "History, 1 March–31 March 1946. Weekly Staff Conference (Notes), 30 March 1946" (Suitland, Md.: National Archives, Record Group 338, Box 80).

33. Third U.S. Army Headquarters, Chief of Staff Section, "Report of Operations, 1 April-30 June 1946," (Suitland, Md.: National Archives, Record Group 338, Box 80): 14.

34. Letter of Dr. Arthur Volz, personal communication to author.

35. Third U.S. Army Headquarters, Chief of Staff Section, "Report of Operations, 1 January-31 March 1946." "History, 1 March-31 March 1946, Weekly Staff Conference (Notes)," March 30 1946. (Suitland, Md.: National Archives, Record Group 338, Box 80).

36. Dr. Arthur Volz, personal communication to author.

37. Morris J. MacGregor, Jr., *Integration of the Armed Forces:* 206.

38. Ibid.: 208.

39. Ulysses Grant Lee, *The Employment of Negro Troops: Special Studies, United States Army in World War II.* (Washington, D.C.: Office of the Chief of Military History, 1966): 276–281.

40. Similar experiences of black soldiers consorting with prostitutes in unhygienic, unregulated environments can be found in places as far away as Hawaii. Sherie Mershon and Steven Schlossman, *Foxholes and Color Lines:* 88.

41. Morris J. MacGregor, Jr., *Integration of the Armed Forces:* 207.

42. "In one instance, the white commander of a black antiaircraft unit even 'posted a notice to the effect that any type of association with white women would be considered rape, the penalty for which was death.'" Sherie Mershon and Steven Schlossman, *Foxholes and Color Lines:* 87. Citing Phillip McGuire, *He Too Spoke for Democracy: Judge Hastie, World War II and the Black Soldier* (New York: Greenwood Press, 1988): 88–9.

43. Third U.S. Army Headquarters, "Report of Operations for the Close-Out Period, 1 January–15 February 1947" (Suitland, Md.: National Archives, Record Group 338, Box 80): 41.

44. Third U.S. Army Headquarters, "Report of Operations for the Quarterly Period 1 April–30 June 1946" (Suitland, Md.: National Archives, Record Group 338, Box 80): 45.

45. Sherie Mershon and Steven Schlossman, *Foxholes and Color Lines:* 88–9.

46. Morris J. MacGregor, Jr., *Integration of the Armed Forces:* 208.

47. Ibid.: 206–7.

48. Ibid.: 209.

49. Ibid.: 210.

50. Ibid.: 179.

51. Third U.S. Army Headquarters, "Report of Operations for the Quarterly Period 1 April–30 June 1946": 36.

52. Ibid.: 51.

53. Third U.S. Army Headquarters, "History of the Command Section for the Period 1 to July 1946" (Suitland, Md.: National Archives, Record Group 338, Box 67): 1.

54. Ibid.: 2.

55. Ibid.: 44.

Chapter IV

1. Edward N. Peterson, *The American Occupation of Germany: Retreat to Victory:* 9–10.

2. Harold Zink, *American Military Government in Germany:* 37.
3. Earl F. Ziemke, "Improvising Stability and Change in Postwar Germany," in *Americans as Proconsuls,* Robert Wolfe (ed.): 64.
4. John Gimbel, *A German Community under American Occupation:* 40. See Edward N. Peterson, *The American Occupation of Germany: Retreat to Victory:* 271–338.
5. Harold Zink, *American Military Government in Germany:* 31.
6. Ibid.: 36. Frederiksen notes that redeployment stripped the U.S. Army in Germany of the best equipment—much of which was never moved to the Pacific, but rather became "lost" in European warehouses, or was "appropriated by American soldiers". Oliver J. Frederiksen, *The American Military Occupation of Germany, 1944–1953:* 49.
7. "If there is any military unit where the adage that a soldier is supposed to let his officers do the thinking applies it is certainly not military government." Harold Zink, *American Military Government in Germany:* 37.
8. John Gimbel, *A German Community under Occupation:* 44.
9. Earl F. Ziemke, "Improvising Stability and Change in Postwar Germany," in *Americans as Proconsuls,* Robert Wolfe (ed.): 64.
10. Ibid.: 64.
11. Oliver J. Frederiksen, *The American Military Occupation of Germany, 1944–1953:* 53.
12. United States Army Forces in Europe, "Occupation" (n.p., n.d.): 6.
13. "No other occupation force was as methodical as the United States." Edward N. Peterson, *The American Occupation of Germany: Retreat to Victory:* 139.
14. Ibid.: 140.
15. Earl F. Ziemke, *The U.S. Army Occupation of Germany, 1944–1946:* 60.
16. Edward N. Peterson, *The American Occupation of Germany: Retreat to Victory:* 140–1. Interestingly, Secretary of the Treasury, Robert Morgenthau, also saw little use for denazification. His perspective was, however, that the Germans were too incorrigible to change their characters.
17. Ibid.: 142.
18. Harold Zink, *American Military Government in Germany:* 241.
19. Edward N. Peterson, *The American Occupation of Germany: Retreat to Victory:* 145.
20. Ibid.: 142.
21. Ibid.: 143.
22. Ibid.
23. Ibid.: 144.
24. This law declared that all pre-1937 Nazi Party members were automatically guilty. Ibid.: 148.

25. Ibid.: 148.
26. Ibid.: 151.
27. Ibid.: 150.
28. William Griffith, "The Denazification Program in the U.S. Zone of Germany," Ph.D. dissertation, Harvard University, 1950: 105.
29. Edward N. Peterson, *The American Occupation of Germany: Retreat to Victory:* 150.
30. Ibid.: 176.
31. Jean Edward Smith (ed.), *The Papers of Lucius Clay: Germany, 1945–1949* (Bloomington: Indiana University Press, 1974): 272.
32. Ibid.
33. According to Peterson, the elections were successful in the sense that there was large voter participation and centrist parties were largely supported. Edward N. Peterson, *The American Occupation of Germany: Retreat to Victory:* 176.
34. Earl F. Ziemke, *The U.S. Army in the Occupation of Germany:* 31.
35. U.S. Senate, Subcommittee of the Committee on Military Affairs, 79th Congress, First Session, Subcommittee of the Committee on Military Affairs, "Hearings: Elimination of German Resources for War," June 22, 1945 (Washington, D.C.: GPO, 1945): 152 and 189.
36. Without further controls, of course, it would always be possible to borrow funds to facilitate the production of reparation goods or even to buy assets for delivery elsewhere.
37. The transfer of some of the capital equipment from the West was not really supposed to be a "gift." The Soviets had agreed to provide food, coal, and other commodities in return for 15 percent of the surplus capital equipment in the West that it would receive. The other 10 percent would be granted free to the Soviet Union. John H. Backer, *The Decision to Divide Germany: American Foreign Policy in Transition* (Durham, N.C.: Duke University Press, 1978): 88–106. In addition, Secretary of State Byrnes accepted the Soviet decision to permit Poland to administer the territory between the Eastern and Western branches of the Neisse until a peace treaty once and for all settled the boundary question. This decision recognized the de-facto Polish annexation of the most expansive agricultural territories that had been under the control of the German Reich.
38. James F. Byrnes, *Speaking Frankly* (New York: Harper, 1947): 83.
39. Alec Cairncross, *The Price of War: British Policy on German Reparations* (New York: Basil Blackwell, 1986): 10.
40. John Lewis Gaddis, *The United States and the Origins of the Cold War* (New York: Columbia University Press, 1972): 239.

41. "We were not making the mistake again of exacting reparations and then lending the money to pay for them." Harry Truman, *Memoirs,* Vol. I: *Year of Decisions* (Garden City: Doubleday, 1955): 411.

42. Lieutenant Colonel John W. Watson, Memorandum to Brigade General William H. Draper, Jr., "Economic Situation, U.S. Sector Berlin," October 26, 1945 (Suitland, Md.: National Archives, Record Group 260, Box 4).

43. Foreign Trade Office, Trade and Commerce Section Office of Military Government (U.S. Zone) "Monthly Report—United States Zone: German Exports, Border Trade, Frontier Control" and Military Government of Germany (U.S. Zone) "Monthly Report of the Military Governor U.S. Zone May 1945–30 November 1946: Trade Commerce (cumulative review)" (Suitland, Md.: National Archives, Record Group 260, Box 34).

44. Captain Thompson H. Boyd, Jr., GEC/ECON, Office of Military Government (U.S. Zone) "Weekly Paragraph Report," December 12, 1945 (Suitland, Md.: National Archive, Record Group 260, Box 6).

45. Trade and Commerce Branch, Memorandum by Colonel Frank T. Balke, Office of Military Government (U.S. Zone), "Memorandum: Dollar Payment for Danish Seeds to be Imported into the U.S. Zone," December 6, 1945 (Suitland, Md.: National Archives, Record Group 260, Box 6).

46. Memorandum, from Director, Industry Branch to Director, Trade and Commerce Branch, "Interzonal Transfers," August 29, 1945 (Suitland, Md.: National Archives, Record Group 260, Box 5).

47. Memorandum from Director, Industry Division, OMGUS, to Chief, Industry Branch, G-5. USFET, "Transfer between Zones in Interim Period," August 29, 1945. (Suitland, Md.: National Archives, Record Group 260, Box 5).

48. Memorandum from Lieutenant Colonel Stanley Andrews, Assistant Chief Food and Agriculture, USFET, to Director-General, Food and Agriculture Branch, Military Government/Economics 6, British Army of the Rhine, "Inter-Zonal Livestock Movement," November 10, 1945 (Suitland, Md.: National Archives, Record Group 260, Box 26).

49. The French authorities did not join the American and British Zones' plans immediately. France's policy toward the occupation population was more similar to that of the Soviets. The French wished to get as much as possible out of the Zone in order to rebuild their own economy. American and German officials in Wiesbaden suggested "that the French expected 40,000 marks worth of goods to be sent into their zone for every 10,000 marks value of goods which they sent out." "Notes on Meeting with U.S. Military Government and German Land Officials, Wiesbaden," October 29, 1945 (Suitland, Md.: National Archives, Record Group 260, Box 16).

50. Memorandum from Deputy Director, Industry Division to Director, Industry Division, "Matters Which Might Be Mentioned at Directors Meeting," September 9, 1945 (Suitland, Md.: National Archives, Record Group 260).

51. Memorandum from S.G. Wennberg to General Draper, "Central Administrative Departments Committee," December 13, 1945 (Suitland, Md.: National Archives, Record Group 260, Box 16).

52. Memorandum from Captain Thompson H. Boyd, Jr., Executive Officer, Trade and Commerce Branch, Economics Division, USFET, to Executive Officer, Economics Division, Office of Military Government (U.S. Zone), "Weekly Report," January 2, 1946 (Suitland, Md.: National Archives, Record Group 260, Box 6).

53. See, for example, the document produced by the OMGUS staff that envisages the continuing of wartime economic controls in cooperation with the Soviet Union. J. Taylor and Harry Gabeman, Industry Division, OMGUS, "Comparison of German Industrial Controls with the United States Materials Control Plan" (Suitland, Md.: National Archives, Record Group 260, Box 11).

54. U.S. House of Representatives, *Session Hearings of the Committee, 1943–50, Volume II: Problems of World War II and Its Aftermath, Part II* (Washington, D.C.: GPO, 1976): 534.

55. U.S. House of Representatives, Subcommittee of the Committee on Appropriations, 79th Congress, First Session, "Hearings: Military Establishment Appropriation Bill for 1946" (Washington, D.C.: GPO, 1945): 52–3. As late as May 25, 1945, Major General John H. Hildring, the director of the War Department's Civil Affairs Division, testified before a House of Representatives subcommittee that the Army was proposing to *reduce* the distribution of essential goods to the German population in the American Zone during 1946.

56. Allied Control Authority, Directorate of Economics, Level of Industry Committee, *A Minimum German Standard of Living in Relation to the Level of Industry,* Memorandum by U.S. Member, September 17, 1945 (Suitland, Md.: National Archives, Record Group 260, Box 2): 3–4 and 14.

57. Allied Control Authority, Directorate of Economics, Level of Industry Committee, The Future Level of German Industry, Memorandum by U.S. Member, January 28, 1946 (Berlin: Office of Military Government, U.S.): 2.

58. Alec Cairncross, *The Price of War: British Policy on German Reparations:* 109.

59. Benjamin Ulysses Ratchford and William D. Ross, *Berlin Reparations Assignment: Round One of the German Peace Settlement* (Chapel Hill: University of North Carolina Press, 1947): 31.

60. Ibid.: 174.
61. Alec Cairncross, *The Price of War:* 122–26.
62. Benjamin Ulysses Ratchford and William D. Ross, *Berlin Reparations Assignment:* 171.
63. Edward N. Peterson, *The American Occupation of Germany: Retreat to Victory:* 68.
64. John Lewis Gaddis, *The United States and the Origins of the Cold War:* 328–9. John Gimbel, *The Origins of the Marshall Plan:* 144.
65. Before becoming Chief of the Industry Branch, Boyd had been Professor of Economic Geography, Colorado School of Mines. Benjamin Ulysses Ratchford and William D. Ross, *Berlin Reparations Assignment:* 87–8.
66. Office of Military Government, (U.S. Zone) Industry Division, Office of Military Government for Germany (U.S.), "Report on Industrial Disarmament, 1945" (Suitland, Md.: National Archives, Record Group 260, Box 1): cover letter.
67. Ibid.: 3.
68. Ibid.: 3, 8, and 10.
69. Ibid.: 12–13.
70. Ibid.: 15–16.

Chapter V

1. Memorandum, General Dwight Eisenhower to Colonel H. H. Newman, Assistant Adjutant General, October 16, 1945 (Suitland, Md.: National Archives, Record Group 332, Box 1).
2. Ernest N. Harmon, *Memoirs* (Carlisle, Pa.: U.S. Army Military History Institute, Ernest Harmon Collection, Box 3): 177–8.
3. The Third Army's Report of Operations comments on the effects of one of General McNarney's first efforts to improve discipline. "The change that most adversely affected troop feeling within the quarter was the introduction of close order drill to follow the reveille formation each morning." Third U.S. Army, Headquarters, "Report of Operations, 1 January–31 March 1946" (Suitland, Md.: National Archives, Record Group 338, Box 80): 96.
4. Office of the Provost Marshal, United States Constabulary, *Statistical Report of Operations,* March 1947 (Carlisle, Pa.: U.S. Army Military History Institute, Ernest Harmon Collection, Box 3).
5. Major James M. Snyder, Cavalry, *United States Constabulary: The Establishment and Operation of the United States Constabulary* (Historical Sub-Section G–3, United States Constabulary: 1947): 217 and 221, in The Halley G. Maddox

Papers, Box labeled "U.S. Constabulary, 3 October 1945–30 June 1946" (Carlisle, Pa.: U.S. Army Military History Institute).

6. The 100th Infantry Division Papers, files of Private First Class Raymond O. Denman, Jr. (Carlisle, Pa.: U.S. Army Military History Institute, n.d.).

7. Third U.S. Army, Headquarters, "Report of Operations for the Quarterly Period 1 October–31 December 1946" (Suitland, Md.: National Archives, Record Group 338, Box 80): 86.

8. Third U.S. Army, Headquarters, "Report of Operations for the Close-Out Period, 1 January–15 February 1947" (Suitland, Md.: National Archives, Record Group 338, Box 80): 45.

9. Third U.S. Army, Headquarters, "Report of Operations, 1 October–31 December 1945" (Suitland, Md.: National Archives, Record Group 338, Box 80): 67.

10. Third U.S. Army, Headquarters, "Report of Operations, 1 January–31 March 1946": 95.

11. Ibid.: 86.

12. Ibid.: 40.

13. Third U.S. Army, Headquarters, "Report of Operations for the Period, 1 October–31 December 1945": 68.

14. Third U.S. Army, Headquarters, G-3 Section, "Report for the Month of November 1945" (Suitland, Md.: National Archives, Record Group 338, Box 67): 8–9.

15. Third U.S. Army, Headquarters, G-3 Section, "Report for the Month of December 1945" (Suitland, Md.: National Archives, Record Group 338, Box 67): 7.

16. Third U.S. Army, Headquarters, "Report of Operations for the Period 1 October–31 December 1945": 105.

17. Ibid.: 77.

18. Third U.S. Army, Headquarters, "Report of Operations for the Period 1 January–31 March 1946": 82–3.

19. Third U.S. Army, Headquarters, G-3 Section, "Report for the Month of January 1946" (Suitland, Md.: National Archives, Record Group 338, Box 67): 13.

20. Ibid.: 83–4.

21. Ibid.: 85.

22. Third U.S. Army, Headquarters, "Report of Operations for the Period 1 April–30 June 1946" (Suitland, Md.: National Archives, Record Group 338, Box 80): 77.

23. Third U.S. Army, Headquarters, "Report of Operations for the Period 1 January–31 March 1946": 86.

24. Third U.S. Army, Headquarters, "Report of Operations for the Period 1

April–30 June 1946": 69 and "Report of Operations for the Period 1 July–30 September 1946" (Suitland, Md.: National Archives, Record Group 338, Box 80): 92.

25. Third U.S. Army, Headquarters, "Report of Operations for the Quarterly Period 1 October–31 December 1946": 86.

26. Third U.S. Army, Headquarters, "Army Commander's Weekly Staff Conference (Notes), 9 March 1946" (Suitland, Md.: National Archives, Record Group 338, Box 66): 7.

27. U.S. Army Forces in the European Theater, "Occupation," 1946: 10.

28. Ibid.: 11.

29. Third U.S. Army, Headquarters, "Report of Operations for the Period 1 October–31 December 1945": 80.

30. Third U.S. Army, Headquarters, "Report of Operations for the Period 1 January–31 March 1946": 59.

31. Ibid.: 92.

32. Third U.S. Army, Headquarters, "Report of Operations for the Period 1 April–30 June 1946": 75.

33. Third U.S. Army, Headquarters, "Report of Operations for the Period 1 October–31 December 1946": 89–90.

34. Third U.S. Army, Headquarters, "Report of Operations for the Period 1 January–31 March 1946": 92–3.

35. Third U.S. Army, Headquarters, "Report of Operations for the Period 1 October–31 December 1946": 90.

36. Third U.S. Army, Headquarters, "Report of Operations for the Period 1 April–30 June 1946": 75.

37. Third U.S. Army, Headquarters, "Report of Operations for the Period 1 October–31 December 1945": 78.

38. Third U. S. Army, Headquarters, "Report of Operations for the Period 1 January–31 March 1946": 89.

39. Ibid.: 88–9.

40. Third U.S. Army, Headquarters, "Report of Operations for the Period 1 April–30 June 1946": 72.

41. Ibid.

42. Third U.S. Army, Headquarters, "Report of Operations for the Period 1 July–30 September 1946": 95–6.

43. Third U.S. Army, Headquarters, "Report of Operations for the Period 1 October–31 December 1946": 88.

44. Ibid.

45. Third U.S. Army, Headquarters, "Report of Operations for the Period 1 October–31 December 1945": 77.

46. Earl F. Ziemke, *The U.S. Army in the Occupation of Germany,* 1944–46: 376.
47. Third U.S. Army, Headquarters, "Report of Operations for the Period 1 April–30 June 1946": 73.
48. Third U.S. Army, Headquarters, "Report of Operations for the Period 1 October–31 December 1945": 77.
49. Third U.S. Army, Headquarters, "Report of Operations for the Period 1 January–31 March 1946": 89.
50. Third U.S. Army, Headquarters, "Report of Operations for the Period 1 October–31 December 1945": 77; "Report of Operations for the Quarterly Period 1 January–31 March 1946": 90; and "Report of Operations for the Period 1 April–30 June 1946": 73.
51. The Third Army's last report continued to express dissatisfaction with the European Theater's efforts to control GI misbehavior. Third U.S. Army, Headquarters, "Report of Operations for the Close-Out Period, 1 January–15 February 1947."
52. Third U.S. Army, Headquarters, Third U.S. Army, "Report of Operations for Period, 1 July–30 September 1946": 29.
53. Ibid: 99.
54. Third U.S. Army, Headquarters, "Report of Operations for the Period 1 January–31 March 1946": 90.
55. Third U.S. Army, Headquarters, "Report of Operations for the Period 1 July–30 September 1946": 30.
56. Third U.S. Army, Headquarters, Adjutant General, "Xmas Party Report," 28 December 1946 (Suitland, Md.: National Archives, Record Group 338, Box 67).
57. Third U.S. Army, Headquarters, "Report of Operations for the Period 1 October–31 December 1946": 92 and 97.
58. Third U.S. Army, Headquarters, "Report of Operations for the Period 1 July–30 September 1946": 2–3.
59. Ibid.

Chapter VI

1 "Picture of the Week," *Life,* Feb. 4, 1946: 24–5. A letter in the Feb. 25, 1946 edition of *Life* from Mrs. James A. Morgan revealed that the demonstration was organized by the "Bring the Dads Back" Club. Mrs. James A. Morgan, Letter to the Editor, *Life,* February 25, 1946: 10.
2. Emily Latimer, Letter to the Editor, *Life,* August 13, 1945: 4. The double standard was alive and well in 1945. Only 6 percent of the public believed that "a woman whose husband is overseas should accept dates with other

men." Here men and women agreed. Seven percent of men thought that such behavior was acceptable, while only 5 percent of women answered affirmatively. See the Gallup Poll results of July 14, 1945 and August 4, 1945 reported in George H. Gallup, *The Gallup Poll: Public Opinion, 1935–1971,* Vol. 1, 1935–1948 (New York: Random House, 1971).

3. Oliver J. Frederiksen, *The American Military Occupation of Germany, 1945–1953:* 120–1.

4. Ibid.

5. "During the first years of the occupation the number of dependents did not rise far above thirty thousand." Ibid.

6. "Such plans will provide, insofar as practicable a standard of living for U.S. troops and their dependents comparable to that in the United States in 1937, and in no case will troops be quartered in barracks below the standard occupied by German troops prior to the war. . . ." Third U.S. Army, Headquarters, G-1 Section, Headquarters, "Report for the Month of December 1945" (Suitland, Md.: National Archives, Record Group 338, Box 65): 7.

7. Oliver J. Frederiksen, *The American Military Occupation of Germany, 1945–1953:* 121.

8. Ibid.: 121–2.

9. Ibid.: 124.

10. Third U.S. Army, Headquarters, "Report of Operations for the Quarterly Period 1 April–30 June 1946" (Suitland, Md.: National Archives, Record Group 338, Box 80): 34.

11. Third U.S. Army, Headquarters, G-1 Section, "Monthly History for April 1946," (Suitland, Md.: National Archives, Record Group 338, Box 67): 3.

12. Third U.S. Army, Headquarters, G-1 Section, Headquarters, "Monthly Histories for March 1946," (Suitland, Md.: National Archives, Record Group 338, Box 67): 11.

13. Third U.S. Army, Headquarters, "Report of Operations for the Quarterly Period 1 July–30 September 1946." (Suitland, Md.: National Archives, Record Group 338, Box 80): 14.

14. Third U.S. Army, Headquarters, "Report of Operations for the Close-Out Period, 1 January–15 February 1947" (Suitland, Md.: National Archives, Record Group 338, Box 80): 27–8.

15. Third U.S. Army, Headquarters, "Report of Operations for the Quarterly Period 1 January–31 March 1946" (Suitland, Md.: National Archives, Record Group 338, Box 80): 62.

16. Third U.S. Army, Headquarters, "Report of Operations for the Quarterly Period 1 October–31 December 1946" (Suitland, Md.: National Archives, Record Group 338, Box 80): 99–100.

17. Third U.S. Army, Headquarters, G-1 Section, "Monthly Historical Reports," June 10, 1946 (Suitland, Md.: National Archives, Record Group 338, Box 67): 4.

18. Third U.S. Army, Headquarters, "Report of Operations for the Quarterly Period 1 October–31 December 1946": 59.

19. "The War Department has advised that no more appropriated funds will be available for procurement of construction materials for the dependents program alone, as opposed to construction materials essential to military requirements, and a program has been approved whereby the United States Zone will be combed in order to obtain from unoccupied damaged buildings such critical items as may be possible for salvage." Ibid.

20. Third U.S. Army, Headquarters, G-1 Section, "Monthly Histories," January 1947 (Suitland, Md.: National Archives, Record Group 338, Box 67): 17–18.

21. Ibid.; 18.

22. Third U.S. Army, Headquarters, "Report of Operations, 1 April–30 June 1946" (Suitland, Md.: National Archives, Record Group 338, Box 80): 87.

23. "U.S. Wives Arrive in Germany: American Families Are Joyously Reunited as Glum Germans Watch," *Life,* May 27, 1946: 55–6.

24. The Army made a strong effort to screen all servants in order to ensure that none were carriers of communicable diseases. "To protect United States military personnel and their dependents from communicable disease, it has been ordered that no household employee be hired, or permitted to continue employment, unless proven free from infection. Immunizations are required and routine physical inspections made." Third U.S. Army, Headquarters, "Report of Operations for the Close-Out Period 1 January–15 February 1947": 73.

25. "Report on the U.S. Occupation of Germany," *Life,* February 10, 1947: 89.

26. For more details, see John Willoughby, "The Sexual Behavior of American GIs During the Early Years of the Occupation of Germany," *The Journal of Military History* 62, January 1998: 155–74.

27. "Speaking of Pictures," *Life,* June 17, 1946: 15. The Army restricted the publication of Don Sheppard's cartoons for fear that they would offend German sensibilities.

28. Franklin M. Davis, Jr., *Came as a Conqueror: The United States Army's Occupation of Germany 1945–1949:* 191.

29. Bud Hutton and Andy Rooney, *Conqueror's Peace: Report to the American Stockholders:* 51.

30. By June 1948, Americans and Germans had contracted 3,500 legal marriages. Oliver J. Frederiksen, *The American Military Occupation of Germany,*

1945–1953: 137. It probably did not hurt matters that the first German woman granted a fiancée visa was Anna Maria Christina Heinke. Heinke's father died in a Nazi concentration camp. Thus, her marriage to Robert Lauenstein of St. Louis could not be cause for worries about Nazi contamination. Bud Hutton and Andy Rooney, *Conqueror's Peace: Report to the American Stockholders,* (New York: Doubleday and Co., 1947): 50.

31. Jean Edward Smith, Lucius D. Clay: An American Life (New York: Henry Holt and Co., 1990): 325.

32. As late as 1949, the German police were still having difficulty controlling drunken GIs in pursuit of young women. Police Chief Drzmilla of Augsburg commented that after the rule prohibiting Americans from visiting German taverns was temporarily lifted, "Most Americans behaved themselves, [but] there were fights, because of girls and drunkenness, in which the German usually was helpless and was thoroughly beaten up." Edward N. Peterson, *The American Occupation of Germany: Retreat to Victory:* 29.

33. Feminist political scientist Cynthia Enloe has argued more generally that the establishment of a foreign base system requires the "delicate adjustment of relations between men and women." The story of postwar Germany indicates that the establishment of family-friendly military bases was necessary for this "delicate adjustment." Cynthia Enloe, *Bananas, Beaches, and Bases: Making Feminist Sense of International Politics:* 67.

34. Morris MacGregor, Jr., *Integration of the Armed Forces 1940–1965:* 188.

35. Ibid.: 185–6.

36. Third U.S. Army, Headquarters, "Notes from Commander's Weekly Staff Conference," 2 November 1946 (Suitland, Md.: National Archives, Record Group 338, Box 67).

37. It is the case, however, that President Truman himself clearly believed that the implementation of his order would require full military integration of the races. Sherie Mershon and Steven Schlossman, *Foxholes and Color Lines: Desegregating the U.S. Armed Forces:* 184.

38. Ibid.: 207.

39. Ibid.

40. Morris MacGregor, Jr., *Integration of the Armed Forces 1940–1965:* 271.

41. Ibid.: 216.

42. Ibid.: 217.

43. Ibid.: 218 and 280.

44. Sherie Mershon and Steven Schlossman, *Foxholes and Color Lines: Desegregating the U.S. Armed Forces:* 73.

45. Ibid.: 141.

46. Ibid.: 142.

47. Ibid.: 143.
48. Ibid.: 178.
49. Ibid.

Chapter VII

1. "Three Occupation Reports," *New York Times,* January 6, 1946, section IV:1.
2. "The German People," *Life,* May 7, 1945: 22.
3. "Grim Europe Faces Winter of Misery," *Life,* January 7, 1946.
4. John Dos Passos, "Americans are Losing the Victory," *Life,* January 7, 1946: 23.
5. Drew Middleton, "Failure in Germany," *Collier's Weekly* 117, February 9, 1946: 13.
6. Edward P. Morgan, "Heels among the Heroes," *Collier's Weekly* 118, October 19, 1946: 16.
7. Ibid.: 14.
8. Ibid.: 108.
9. Memoirs of soldiers during the occupation repeat this theme in many different ways. In his recent autobiography *'Tis,* Frank McCourt writes about the dilemmas he faced when thinking about what he would tell his Irish-American girlfriend about his whoring in Germany:

   > I can't tell her about the excitement I've had with girls in Lenggries and Munich and the refugee camp. She'd be so shocked she might tell her whole family, especially her big brother Liam, and there would be threats on my life.
   > Rappaport says that before you get married it's your obligation to tell the bride about all the things you've done with other girls. Buck says, That's bullshit, the best thing in life is to keep your mouth shut especially with someone you're going to marry. It's like the army, never tell, never volunteer.

   Frank McCourt, *'Tis: A Memoir* (New York: Scribner, 1999): 124.
10. Edward P. Morgan, "Heels among the Heroes," 16.
11. John Dos Passos, "Retreat from Europe," *In the Year of Our Defeat* (Boston: Houghton Mifflin, 1946): 331.
12. Joe Weston, "Life's Reports: The GIs in Le Havre: Americans in France are envoys of Ill Will," *Life:* 20.
13. Ibid.
14. Julian Bach, Jr., *America's Germany: An Account of the Occupation:* 72–3.
15. Janet Hobhouse, *Everybody Who Was Anybody: A Biography of Gertrude Stein* (New York: Putnam, 1975): 223–4.
16. Gertrude Stein, "Off We All Went to See Germany: Germans Should Learn

to be Disobedient and GIs Shouldn't Like Them No They Shouldn't," *Life,* August 6, 1945: 58.

17. Janet Hobhouse, *Everybody Who Was Anybody:* 227.

18. Gertrude Stein, *Brewsie and Willie* (New York: Random House, 1946): 3–4.

19. Ibid.: 5.

20. Ibid.: 6.

21. Ibid.: 13.

22. Ibid.: 19.

23. Ibid.: 26–7.

24. Ibid.: 55–6.

25. Stein suggests in scattered parts of *Brewsie and Willie* that only African American soldiers might emerge from World War II as pioneers. She states that white soldiers are bothered by integration, but not likely to respond violently. One odd aspect of Stein's analysis is that black Americans are becoming pioneers by domesticating themselves in ways that she would otherwise deplore.

"Yeah, it's funny, said Jimmie, the only real pioneering there is in America these days is done by Negroes. They're pioneering, they find new places, new homes, new lives, new ways and they more and more own something, funny, said Jimmie, kind of queer and funny. I dont like it, said Jo. No, said Jimmie. No I dont like it, said Jo, it makes me kind of nervous." Ibid.: 65.

26. Ibid.: 69.

27. Frederick Jackson Turner, "The Significance of the Frontier in American History." *In the Frontier in American History* (New York: Henry Holt and Company, 1958): 3–4.

28. Ibid.: 3.

29. Gertrude Stein, *Brewsie and Willie:* 23.

30. Ibid.: 110–1.

Bibliography

Articles in Books and Journals

Clay, Lucius. "Proconsul of a People, by Another People, for Both Peoples." In *Americans as Proconsuls: United States Military Government in Germany and Japan, 1944–1952,* ed. Robert Wolfe. Carbondale: Southern Illinois Press, 1984.

Collins, Steven. "Disguised Hostility: The German Response to the U.S. Occupation of the Rhineland after the First World War." Presented at Society for Military History Conference. Gettysburg, Penn: May 13, 1995.

Dos Passos, John. "Retreat from Europe." In *In the Year of Our Defeat.* Boston: Houghton Mifflin, 1946.

Iriye, Akira. "The United States as an Occupier." *Reviews in American History* 16, (March 1988): 65–72.

Peterson, Edward N. "The Occupation as Perceived by the Public, Scholars, and Policy Makers." In *Americans as Proconsuls: United States Military Government in Germany and Japan, 1944–1952,* ed. Robert Wolfe. Carbondale: Southern Illinois Press, 1984.

Schrott, Hans-Juergen. "U.S. Forces in Germany, 1946–1955." In *U.S. Military Forces in Europe: The Early Years, 1945–1970,* eds. Simon W. Duke and Wolfgang Krieger. Boulder: Westview Press, 1993.

Turner, Frederick Jackson. "The Significance of the Frontier in American History." In *The Frontier in American History.* New York: Henry Holt and Company, 1958.

Willoughby, John. "The Sexual Behavior of American GIs During the Early Years of the Occupation of Germany." *The Journal of Military History* 62 (January 1998): 155–74.

Ziemke, Earl F. "Improvising Stability and Change in Postwar Germany." In

Americans as Proconsuls: United States Military Government in Germany and Japan, 1944–1952, ed. Robert Wolfe. Carbondale: Southern Illinois Press, 1984.

Ziemke, Earl. F. "The Formulation and Initial Implementation of U.S. Occupation in Germany." In *U.S. Occupation in Europe after World War II: Papers and Reminiscences from the April 23–24, 1976 Conference Held at the George C. Marshall Research Foundation, Lexington, Virginia,* ed. Hans A. Schmitt. Lawrence: The Regents Press of Kansas, 1978.

Books

Abelshauser, Werner. *Wirtschaft in Westdeutschland 1945–1948: Rekonstrucktion und Wachstumsbedingunger in der amerikanischen und britischen Zone.* Stuttgart: Deutsche Verlags-Anstalt, 1975.

Bach, Julian, Jr. *America's Germany: An Account of the Occupation.* New York: Random House, 1946.

Backer, John H. *Priming the German Economy: American Occupational Policies, 1945–48.* Durham, N.C.: Duke University Press, 1971.

Backer, John H. *The Decision to Divide Germany: American Foreign Policy in Transition.* Durham, N.C.: Duke University Press, 1978.

Beever, Antony, and Artemis Cooper, *Paris After the Liberation, 1944–1949.* New York: Doubleday, 1994.

Berube, Allan. *Coming Out Under Fire: The History of Gay Men and Women in World War II.* New York: Free Press, 1990.

Brandt, Allan. *No Magic Bullet: A Social History of Venereal Disease in the United States Since 1880.* New York: Oxford University Press, 1975.

Byrnes, James F. *Speaking Frankly.* New York: Harper, 1947.

Cairncross, Alec. *A Country To Play With: Level of Industry Negotiation in Berlin 1945–46.* Gerrards Cross; Colin Smythe, 1987.

Cairncross, Alec. *The Price of War: British Policy on German Reparations.* New York: Basil Blackwell, 1986.

Churchill, Winston S. *Triumph and Tragedy: The Second World War,* Vol. 6. Boston: Houghton Mifflin, 1953.

Cosmas, Graham A., and Albert E. Cowdry, *Medical Service in the European Theater of Operations: The Medical Department.* Washington, DC: Center of Military History, United States Army, 1992.

Costello, John. *Virtue Under Fire: How World War II Changed Our Social and Sexual Attitudes.* Boston: Little, Brown and Co., 1985.

Dastrup, Boyd L. *Crusade in Nuremberg: Military Occupation, 1945–1949.* Westport, Conn.: Greenwood Press, 1985.

Davis, Franklin M., Jr. *Came as a Conqueror: The United States Occupation of Germany.* New York: Macmillan, 1967.

Enloe, Cynthia. *Bananas, Beaches, and Bases: Making Feminist Sense of International Politics.* Berkeley: University of California Press, 1989.

Frederiksen, Oliver J. *The American Military Occupation of Germany, 1945–1953.* n.p.: Headquarters, United States Army Europe, Historical Division, 1953.

Gaddis, John Lewis. *The United States and the Origins of the Cold War: 1941–1947.* New York: Columbia University Press, 1972.

Gallup, George H., *The Gallup Poll: Public Opinion, 1935–1975,* vol. 1, *1935–1948.* New York: Random House, 1971.

Gimbel, John, *A German Community Under Occupation.* Stanford, Calif.: Stanford University Press, 1961.

Gimbel, John. *The Origins of the Marshall Plan.* Stanford, Calif.: Stanford University Press, 1976.

Grandstaff, Mark. *Foundation of the Force: Air Force Enlisted Personnel Policy, 1907–1956.* Washington, DC: Government Printing Office, 1997.

Griffith, William. "The Denazification Program in the U.S. Zone of Germany." Ph.D. Diss., Harvard University, 1950.

Harmon, Ernest N. *Memoirs.* Carlisle, Pa.: Military History Institute, The Ernest Harmon Collection, n.d., Box 3.

Hobhouse, Janet. *Everybody Who Was Anybody: A Biography of Gertrude Stein.* New York: Putnam, 1975.

Hoover, Calvin. *Memoirs of Capitalism, Communism and Nazism.* Durham, N.C.: Duke University Press, 1965.

Hutton, Bud, and Andy Rooney, *Conquerors' Peace: Report to the American Stockholders.* New York: Doubleday and Co., 1947.

Kennan, George, *Memoirs.* London: Hutchinsons of London, 1968.

Lee, Ulysses Grant. *The Employment of Negro Troops: Special Studies, United States Army in World War II.* Washington, D.C.: Office of the Chief of Military History, 1966.

Leffler, Melvyn P. *A Preponderance of Power: National Security, the Truman Administration, and the Cold War.* Stanford, Calif.: Stanford University Press, 1992.

McCourt, Frank. *'Tis: A Memoir.* New York: Scribner, 1999.

MacGregor, Morris J., Jr. *Integration of the Armed Forces 1940–45.* Washington, D.C.: Center of Military History, 1981.

McGuire, Phillip. *He Too Spoke for Democracy: Judge Hastie, World War II, and the Black Soldier.* New York: Greenwood Press, 1988.

McGuire, Phillip, ed. *Taps for a Jim Crow Army: Letters from Black Soldiers in World War II.* Lexington: University Press of Kentucky, 1993.

Mershon, Sherie, and Steven Schlossman. *Foxholes and Color Lines: Desegregating the U.S. Armed Forces.* Baltimore: The Johns Hopkins University Press, 1998.

Motley, Mary Penich, ed. *The Invisible Soldier: The Experience of the Black Soldier.* Detroit, Mich.: Wayne State University, 1975.

Murphy, Robert. *Diplomat Among Warriors.* Garden City, N.Y.: Doubleday, 1964.

Nalty, Bernard, and Morris J. MacGregor, Jr., eds. *Blacks in the Military: Essential Documents.* Wilmington, Del.: Scholarly Resources, Inc., 1981.

Nelson, Daniel, J. *A History of U.S. Military Forces in Germany.* Boulder, Colo.: Westview Press, 1987.

Peterson, Edward N., *The American Occupation of Germany: Retreat to Victory.* Detroit, Mich.: Wayne State University, 1977.

Ratchford, Benjamin Ulysses, and William D. Ross. *Berlin Reparations Assignment: Round One of the German Peace Settlement.* Chapel Hill, N.C.: University of North Carolina Press, 1947.

Reynolds, David. *Rich Relations: The American Occupation of Britain, 1942–45.* New York: Random House, 1995.

Schaller, Michael. *The American Occupation of Japan: The Origins of the Cold War in Asia.* New York: Oxford University Press, 1985.

Smith, Jean Edward. *Lucius D. Clay: An American Life.* New York: Henry Holt and Co., 1990.

Smith, Jean Edward, ed. *The Papers of Lucius Clay: Germany, 1945–1949.* Bloomington: Indiana University Press, 1974.

Snyder, Major James M. *United States Constabulary: The Establishment and Operation of the United States Constabulary.* n.p.: United States Constabulary, 1947.

Stein, Gertrude. *Brewsie and Willie.* New York: Random House, 1946.

Studies of American Interests in the War and the Peace. New York: Council of Foreign Relations, early 1940s.

Truman, Harry. *Memoirs,* vol. 1, *Year of Decisions.* Garden City, N.Y.: Doubleday, 1955.

White, W.L. *Report on the Germans.* New York: Harcourt, Brace and Co., 1947.

Whitnah, Donald R., and Edgar L. Erickson. *The American Occupation of Austria: Planning and Early Years.* Westport, Conn.: Greenwood Press, 1985.

Wynn, Neil A. *The Afro-American and the Second World War.* New York: Holmes and Meier, 1993.

Ziemke, Earl F. *The U.S. Army in the Occupation of Germany, 1944–46.* Washington, D.C.: Center of Military History, United States, Army, 1985.

Zink, Harold. *American Military Government in Germany.* New York: Macmillan, 1947.

Government Documents and Other Papers

Allied Control Authority, Directorate of Economics, Level of Industry Committee. *A Minimum German Standard of Living in Relation to the Level of Industry.*

Memorandum by U.S. Member, September 17, 1945. Suitland, Md.: National Archives, Record Group 260, Box 2.

Allied Control Authority, Directorate of Economics, Level of Industry Committee, *The Future Level of German Industry.* Memorandum by the U.S. Representative. Berlin: January 28, 1946.

Memorandum, General Dwight Eisenhower to Col. H. H. Newman, Assistant Adjutant General. "Morale Welfare Clip," October 16, 1945. Suitland, Md.: National Archives, Record Group 332, Box 1.

"Notes on Meeting with U.S. Military Government and German Land Officials, Wiesbaden," October 29, 1945. Suitland, Md.: National Archives, Record Group 260, Box 14.

Office of Military Government (U.S. Zone), Foreign Trade Office, Trade and Commerce Section. *Monthly Report—United States Zone: German Exports, Border Trade, Frontier Control.* Suitland, Md.: National Archives, Record Group 260, Box 34.

Office of Military Government (U.S. Zone), Industry Division. *Report on Industrial Disarmament.* Suitland Md.: National Archives, Record Group 260, Box 1.

Office of Military Government (U.S. Zone), Memorandum from Deputy Director, Industry Division, to Director, Industry Division. "Matters Which Might Be Mentioned at Directors Meeting," September 9, 1945. Suitland, Md.: National Archives, Record Group 260, Box 5.

Office of Military Government (U.S. Zone), Memorandum from Director, Industry Branch to Chief, Industry Branch, G–5, USFET. "Transfer between Zones in Interim Period," August 29, 1945. Suitland, Md.: National Archives, Record Group 260, Box 5.

Office of Military Government (U.S. Zone), Memorandum from Director, Industry Branch, to Director, Trade and Commerce Branch, "Interzonal Transfers," August 29 1945. Suitland, Md.: National Archives, Record Group 260, Box 5.

Office of Military Government (U.S. Zone), Memorandum from Lt. Col. Stanley Andrews, Assistant Chief Food and Agriculture, USFET, to Director-General, Food and Agriculture Branch, Military Government/Economics, British Army of the Rhine, "Inter-Zonal Livestock Movement," November 10, 1945. Suitland, Md.: National Archives, Record Group 260, Box 26.

Office of Military Government (U.S. Zone), Memorandum from S. G. Wennberg to General Draper. "Central Administrative Departments Committee," December 13, 1945. Suitland, Md.: National Archives, Record Group 260, Box 16.

Office of Military Government (U.S. Zone), Trade and Commerce Branch, Memorandum by Colonel Frank T. Balke, "Dollar Payment for Danish Seeds to be Imported into the U.S. Zone," December 6, 1945. Suitland, Md.: National Archives, Record Group 260, Box 6.

Office of Military Government (U.S. Zone), "Trade Commerce (Cumulative Review): 8 May 1945–30 November 1946." Suitland, Md.: National Archives, Box 34.

Office of the Provost Marshal, United States Constabulary. *Statistical Report of Operations.* March 1946. Carlisle, Pa.: Military History Institute, The Ernest Harmon Collection, Box 3.

100th Industry Division Papers. Carlisle, Pa.: Military History Institute.

Taylor, J., and Harry Gabeman, Office of Military Government (U.S. Zone), Industry Division. "Comparison of German Industrial Controls with the United States Materials Control Plan." Suitland, Md.: National Archives, Record Group 260, Box 11.

Third U.S. Army, G–1 Section, Various "Monthly Historical Report[s]" Suitland, Md.: National Archives, Record Group 338, Boxes 67 and 68.

Third U.S. Army, Headquarters. "History of the Command Section for the Period 1 to 31 July 1946." Suitland, Md.: National Archives, Record Group 338, Box 67.

Third U.S. Army, Headquarters. "Report of Operations for the Close-Out Period, 1 January–15 February 1947." Suitland, Md.: National Archives, Record Group 338, Box 80.

Third U.S. Army, Headquarters. "Report of Operations for the Quarterly Period, 1 October–31 December 1945." Suitland, Md.: National Archives, Record Group 338, Box 80.

Third U.S. Army, Headquarters. "Report of Operations for the Quarterly Period, 1 January–31 March 1946." Suitland, Md.: National Archives, Record Group 338, Box 80.

Third U.S. Army, Headquarters. Report of Operations for the Quarterly Period, 1 April 1946–30 June 1946. Suitland, Md.: National Archives, Record Group 338, Box 80.

Third U.S. Army, Headquarters. Report of Operations for the Quarterly Period, 1 July–30 September 1946. Suitland, Md.: National Archives, Record Group 338, Box 80.

Third U.S. Army, Headquarters. Report of Operations for the Quarterly Period, 1 October–31 December 1946. Suitland, Md.: National Archives, Record Group 338, Box 80.

Third U.S. Army, Provost Marshal's Section. "Report for the Month of October 1945." Suitland, Md.: National Archives, Record Group 338, Box 78.

Third U.S. Army, Provost Marshal's Section. Various "Report[s] of Operations." Suitland, Md.: National Archives, Record Group 338, Boxes 66 and 67.

U.S. Army Forces in the U.S. European Theater (USFET). *Occupation.*1946.

USFET, Trade and Commerce Branch, Economics Division. Various "Weekly Paragraph Report[s]." Suitland, Md.: National Archives, Record Group 260, Box 6.

U.S. House of Representatives. *Session Hearings of the Committee, 1943–50, Volume II: Problems of World War II and Its Aftermath, Part II.* Washington, D.C.: GPO, 1976.

U.S. House of Representatives, Subcommittee of the Committee on Appropriations 79th Congress, 1st Session. *Hearings: Military Establishment Appropriation Bill for 1946.* Washington, D.C.: GPO, 1945.

U.S. Senate, Subcommittee of the Committee on Military Affairs, 79th Congress, 1st Session. *Hearings: Elimination of German Resources for War.* Washington: GPO, 1945.

U.S. Senate, 80th Congress, First Session on Occupation Currency Transactions. *Hearings before the Committees on Appropriations, Armed Services and Banking and Currency.* Washington, D.C.: GPO, 1947.

Watson, John W. Memorandum to Brig. General William H. Draper, Jr., "Economic Situation, U.S. Sector Berlin," October 26, 1945. Suitland, Md.: National Archives, Record Group 260, Box 4.

Popular Magazine and Newspaper Articles

"Americans Steal Hessian Jewels," *Life,* June 24, 1946.

Dos Passos, John. "Americans Are Losing the Victory," *Life,* January 7, 1946.

"Fraternization: The Word Takes On A Brand-New Meaning In Germany," *Life,* July 2, 1945.

"German Girls: U.S. Army Boycott Fails To Stop GIs From Fraternizing With Them," *Life,* July 23, 1945.

"GI Gang Seized in Boxcar: Directed Freight Robberies from Swank Rail Hideout in Germany," *New York Times,* January 5, 1946: 7.

"Grim Europe Faces Winter of Misery," *Life,* January 7, 1946.

Latimer, Emily. Letter to the Editor, *Life,* August 13, 1945.

"*Life* Spends a Day With a GI Occupying Germany," *Life*

"*Life* Visits a German University," *Life,* August 19, 1946.

Long, Tania. "The Longing for a New Fuehrer: German Women Are Bitter , Hostile, and Fearful of the Future; Yet They Are Still Steeped in Nazi Poison," *New York Times Sunday Magazine,* December 9, 1945.

Middleton, Drew. "Failure in Germany," *Collier's Weekly* 117, February 9, 1946.

Morgan, Edward P. "Heels Among the Heroes," *Collier's Weekly* 118, October 19, 1946.

Neill, John. "Vooli Voo, Mamzelle: GIs in Paris Solve Love and Language Problems," *Life,* April 30, 1945.

Neville, Robert. "Army Requisitions: US Soldiers Appropriated Everything in Sight,"

Life, April 8, 1946.

"Picture of the Week," *Life,* February 4, 1946.

Singer, Theodore. Letter to the Editor, *New York Times,* Nov. 30, 1945: 12.

Slatoff, Walter J. "GI Morals in Germany," *The Nation,* May 13, 1946.

"Speaking of Pictures," *Life,* June 17, 1946.

Stein, Gertrude. "Off We All Went to See Germany: Germans Should Learn to be Disobedient and GIs Shouldn't Like Them No They Shouldn't," *Life,* August 6, 1945.

"The German People," *Life,* May 7, 1945.

"The Nazi State Dissolves," *Life,* April 9, 1945.

"Three Occupation Reports," *New York Times,* January 6, 1946, Section IV: 1.

"U.S. Prestige Drops after GI Protests: High Officers Say Occupation of Germany is Affected—McNarney Urges Halt," *New York Times,* January 13, 1946: 1.

"U.S. Wives Arrive in Germany: American Families Are Joyously Reunited as Glum Germans Watch," *Life,* May 27, 1946.

Weston, Joe. "*Life's* Reports: The GIs in Le Havre: American in France Are Envoys of Ill Will, *Life,* December 10, 1945.

Weston, Joe. "We Wanna Go Home," *Life,* January 21, 1946.

Miscellaneous

Volz, Arthur G. "Report of Liaison and Security Office." Provided by Dr. Volz to author.

Index

186   *Index*